Football Clichés

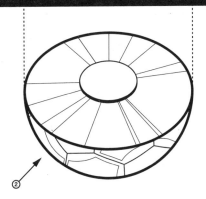

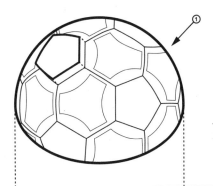

Football
Clichés

A speculative effort, from distance, to translate the curious language of football

Adam Hurrey

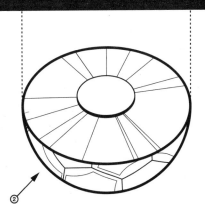

headline

First published in 2014 by
Headline Publishing Group

ISBN 978 1 4722 2038 7

Typeset in Plantin and Helvetica
Designed and illustrated by
James Edgar at
Post98design.co.uk

Printed and bound by
CPI Group (UK) Ltd, Croydon, CR0 4YY

FSC

Headline Publishing Group
An Hachette UK Company
338 Euston Road
London NW1 3BH

www.headline.co.uk
www.hachette.co.uk

To Mum, Dad, Ollie and family, Marc, Andy Townsend and the wonderful Luce, without all of whom this book would probably have been written by somebody else.

Contents

Early Doors

It's not quite clear exactly when a cold, wet night in Stoke replaced one in Rochdale as the quintessentially English benchmark of footballing aptitude, or when sickly parrots and being beyond the orbit of the moon became so passé as metaphors for failure and glory respectively.

Why is football so fond of a cliché? For 150 years, it's been somebody's job to relay what happens within the ninety minutes of a match and, as that coverage now reaches saturation point, a reliable formula for succinct description of the sport has become vital.

Cliché has a perhaps unhelpfully negative connotation. It implies a lack of original thought, of stifling stereotype, and the language of football can certainly be guilty of both of these. On the other hand, football clichés are a leveller – enabling conversation between those relative novices who believe the problem with Arsenal is that they try and walk the ball in and those who feel it's a little more complicated than that. Many clichés, in any subject, qualify as such because they are overwhelmingly true. Yes, just before half-time *is* a good time to score a goal. When isn't it a good time? Well, actually, you can *score too early*. Words like *diminutive, derisory, pulsating* and *profligate* sit with almost absurd comfort in the footballing vernacular, while I struggle to recall anyone using the word *aplomb* in any other context than a well-taken goal.

Also, the heavy reliance on football's stock phrases (by players, fans, journalists and broadcasters alike) can often hide their inventiveness. In a century and a half, nothing has encapsulated the unpredictable swings of a football match more succinctly than *a game of two halves* and yet this eventually grew so hackneyed that it became a cliché to denounce it as a cliché.

Unsurprisingly, for a game whose traditional appreciation of irony extends to a player scoring against an old club, football has taken a long time to become self-aware. The proverbial *good touch for a big man* (despite not featuring in any ancient proverb I'm aware of) enjoyed an unusually short shelf-life before finally becoming impossible to use without a knowing wink. Commentators increasingly prefix their accepted wisdom with 'well, it's the old cliché, isn't it?' and players almost apologetically declare that they 'know it's a cliché' before they insist that they will be *taking every game as it comes*.

The football cliché has become my personal obsession. I find some infuriating, some charming and others waging a perpetual war against logic. At certain points while watching a game, I felt I could predict what was about to come out of the co-commentator's mouth, just as he paused to go through his mental filing cabinet to find the appropriate observation. It was this complicated relationship with the instinctive language of the sport that inspired me to start a blog called *Football Clichés* eight years ago, followed by the Twitter account in 2010 and, finally, this book you're reading now.

It quickly emerged that football clichés were not limited to trite words and hyberbolic metaphors. This was about gestures, mannerisms and patterns of behaviour whose origin – sometimes fellow fans, but mostly players and managers – was markedly clear. This book, in its unashamedly pedantic way, attempts to document every established piece of body language, every hypertruth, every grammatical oddity and every unwritten rule of football.

Not every cliché is indigenous to football but many have been commandeered, butchered and shoehorned into the lexicon because, like James Milner or a strong wall at a free kick, *they do a job*. Their mindless repetition in a football setting takes them further away from their original context – heaven knows what an actual *slide rule* looks like – and this alone makes them worthy of scrutiny. If the word 'clichés' suggests this is a sighing trawl through football's lazy thought and dull phraseology, well, there's certainly plenty of that. But there's ample room for celebration too. Football's innate drama lends itself to wonderfully colourful and evocative language, while its on-pitch stresses continue to elicit the purest, most honest displays of emotion from modern players who otherwise occupy themselves with gamesmanship, deception and self-interest.

As the autopilot coverage of football reaches its uncritical mass, it is perhaps right to embrace its idioms and idiosyncrasies and recognise them as a crucial part of the game. The next fourteen chapters will seek to uphold the football clichés that make some sort of sense, dissect the ones that really don't and, ultimately, justify a childhood spent miming along to John Motson and Barry Davies on worn-out VHS goals compilations.

Adam Hurrey, June 2014

They All Count: 101 Ways to Score a Goal (or Not)

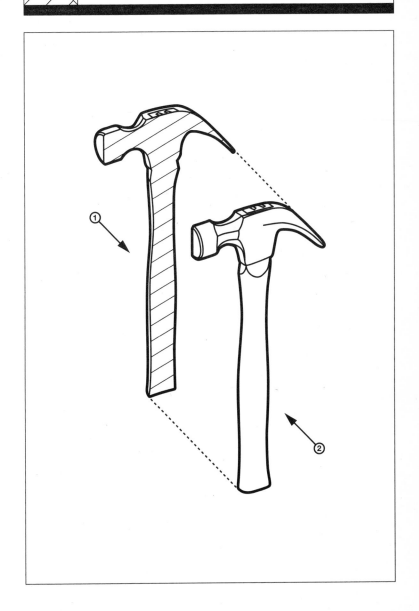

home
/həʊm/

noun
1. the place where one lives
permanently, especially as a member
of a family or household.

adverb
1. into the goal.

1. They All Count: 101 Ways to Score a Goal (or Not)

Goalscorers always insist that it's the three points that matter most, but their individual achievement remains the most fundamental act in association football. There are surely more words and phrases dedicated to goalscoring attempts, successful or otherwise, than any other aspect of the game.

The curious use of the word *home* to describe the act of the ball going into the goal (by means of an *effort*, a *try* or a *pop*, to name but a few) suggests that the goal is where it belongs, and that the act of goalscoring serves to deliver the ball to its rightful place in the back of the *onion bag*.

Ways to Score a Goal

1. Fired

A powerful shot. Its height or range is not important, but its trajectory ought to be straight. Often a way of breaking the deadlock, as the goalscorer fires his team into the lead. This is the first of many firearm-inspired scoring methods in this list.

2. Drilled

Just as forceful as firing, but this time characterised by its relative lack of height – these are *daisy cutters* with extra oomph. Drilled shots invariably find the corner, but this is not mandatory.

3. **Rifled**

A more refined variation of drilling but with more authoritative connotations. Apart from untidy burglars, the verb to *rifle* is almost entirely exclusive to football.

4. **Thundered**

Suitable for describing shots travelling above the ground, which either go in or strike against *the woodwork*.

5. **Hammered**

So evocative a term for powerful long-range efforts that it even extends to players' nicknames, such as German midfielders Jörg 'The Hammer' Albertz and Thomas 'Der Hammer' Hitzlsperger, neither of whom *needed a second invitation* to shoot during their time in British football.

6. **Powered**

A less popular verb, lacking the sheer vividity of the aforementioned blockbusters.

7. **Slammed**

A technique that's often aided aesthetically by the ball being hit into the ground on its way into the net. Suitable for high-velocity goalscoring from close- to mid-range.

8. **Rammed**

The slightly vulgar twin brother of *slammed.*

9. **Blasted**

Surprisingly uncommon, perhaps due to its disregard for technique, but undeniably powerful. Other explosive-themed finishes are the...

10. **Exocet** or the...

11. **Howitzer**

12. **Driven**

Sacrificing some power for unerring direction, drives are distinctly long-range affairs. Estimating the approximate yardage is an optional extra, and you only need to be accurate to the nearest five yards.

13. **Arrowed**

Strictly long-range and top-corner only.

14. **Thumped**

If a *thumping* takes place from close-range and/or thanks to a goalkeeping *howler*, it may well be *gleefully* undertaken. As with a *hammering*, this act of blunt trauma can also be applied to an entire scoreline, should the margin of victory be sufficiently comprehensive.

15. **Lashed**

An instinctive act, somewhat lacking in finesse, but nevertheless useful when loitering in the penalty area.

16. **Smashed**

Largely disappearing from view as a goalscoring verb, perhaps after its unfortunate reappropriation by Richard Keys. Still a woodwork-worthy term, however.

17. Belted

Old-fashioned, like *English No. 9s, shoulder-charges* or *cup-ties, belters* are at home at any level of the football pyramid.

18. Crashing header

Requires some collateral damage in the process, ideally an *overprotected goalkeeper,* as the fearless goalscorer gets a run on his markers to head home. *Crashing headers* overwhelmingly have a downward trajectory, which will be pointed out as a lesson for *any youngsters watching at home.*

19. Towering header

Equal in altitude to the *crashing header,* thanks to a *prodigious leap* comparable to that of a proverbial *salmon,* but not boasting the same level of physical devastation.

20. Nodded

Usually *the simplest of tasks* from close range – an aerial tap-in, if you will.

21. Glancing header

A slow-motion replay delight, as the ball skims deftly off the goalscorer's head and into the far corner.

22. Bullet header

A maximum-velocity header, often making use of the power of the cross that supplied it. Likely to be scored past a goalkeeper who, rather unhelpfully, is *rooted to the spot.*

23. Stooping header

Not high enough to be a *towering header,* nor low enough to require a...

24. Diving header

An art form, perfected in the 1980s by the likes of Keith Houchen and Andy Gray. May require the head to be bravely put *where the boots are flying*.

25. Guided

Cemented as a goalscoring verb by its inclusion in the text commentary of *Championship Manager '93*, but it remains vague. It suggests some degree of craft and composure with either the foot or the head, perhaps taking advantage of the pace of the cross that created the chance.

26. With aplomb

A word commandeered almost exclusively for use in football. Finishing with *aplomb* requires both neatness and style, while remaining magnanimous in comparison to the...

27. Impudent chip

Impudence is best displayed by *diminutive* forwards such as Lionel Messi, at the expense of *stranded* goalkeepers.

28. Audacious lob

The *audacity* of a lob is directly proportional to the distance from goal of its origin.

29. Flicked

Varying in complexity within the six-yard box, almost at any height. A flick is often all that a *teasing cross* requires to succeed.

30. Backheeled

Frequently *cheeky* in general play, but possibly *outrageous* if trying to score from one.

31. Dinked

A snack-sized version of the *impudent chip*, necessitated by an onrushing goalkeeper.

32. Passed

A finish, notable for its nervelessness, which may confound those whose job it is to maintain pass-completion statistics.

33. Caressed

A more romantic take on *passing* the ball in. About as tender as goalscoring gets.

34. Slotted

Ably demonstrated by *natural finishers*, when they find themselves with *only the goalkeeper to beat*.

35. Steered

The lower-body equivalent of the *glancing header*, perhaps. Has enough bend to evade the goalkeeper's dive, but not quite the same amount of arc as it would if it were...

36. Curled

Often *delightfully* performed, beating a dive from the goalkeeper that may only be described as *despairing*.

37. Swept

Swiftly converted from a grounded position, at close range, taking full advantage of a cross delivered into the *corridor of uncertainty*.

38. Turned in

Involves the proverbial *sixpence*, as the goalscorer swivels to score from close range.

39. Stabbed

Not as violent as it suggests, but an ideal form of instinctive, close-combat scoring of a vital goal. Requires more power than a goal that is merely...

40. Prodded, or

41. Poked

42. Stroked

Like *passing* it in, this requires the sort of composure traditionally found on the Continent. *Stroking* the ball home is also an option from the penalty spot.

43. In off the backside

The hypothetical method by which *misfiring* strikers can end a *goal drought* that has, in turn, been measured in games, then hundreds of minutes and then, knife-twistingly, in hours.

44. Deflected

Be it *slight*, *huge* or *wicked*, a deflection should *take nothing away* from the goalscorer, even if it contributed almost entirely to *wrong-footing* the opposing keeper.

45. Own goals (of any sort)

Usually the result of an understandably desperate, last-ditch attempt at an interception. In these cynical times, a defender who is said to have *contrived to turn the ball into his own goal* risks being viewed with undeserved suspicion. Oddly, *own goals* frequently involve the scorer being *credited* with *putting through* his own net. Unfortunate own-goal scorers always have the chance to *atone for* their error by scoring at the right end (and, therefore, *scoring at both ends*), even if both goals are literally scored at the same end of the pitch. A confusing concept all round.

46. Scrambled

The best *goalmouth scrambles* are *almighty* ones, especially if they incorporate a brief period of *pinball* in the box.

47. Bundled

Slightly less dramatic than a *scrambled* effort, but not without controversy. *Bundled* efforts may involve *a suspicion of handball* or *a hint of a foul*, both of which sound like an Agatha Christie novella.

48. Plundered

Now almost extinct. Long-retired *journeyman* strikers were said to have *plundered* their career goal tallies – suggesting they were genuine, *fox-in-the-box poachers*.

49. Notched

Another wide-ranging term for the simple act of *getting on the scoresheet*. Supposedly derived from the late nineteenth-century practice of marking notches on the goalposts to keep score.

50. Netted

With the increasing
obsolescence of the *onion
bag,* less colourful references
to the humble goalnet
continue to suffice. To be
absolutely clear, though, the
ball need not hit the goalnet
to count as being *netted.*

51. Bagged

It is acceptable to store a
single goal in a bag, but it is
more commonly braces or
hat-tricks (*quickfire* or
otherwise) that are *bagged.*

52. Tapped

Much like the *nodded* header,
tap-ins represent one of the
easiest goals a striker will ever
score, and are therefore
unlikely to make it into his
scrapbook.

53. Converted

Best used for penalties that
are scored in a tidy, unfussy
manner – no *impudent*
Panenkas or short run-ups
welcome here, thanks.

54. Dispatched

Bringing satisfaction to
no-frills goalscorers and
online purchasers for many
years now. Dispatching is
often completed *with the
minimum of fuss,* begging the
question: what does a goal
scored with the maximum
of fuss look like?

55. Buried

A great (low-altitude)
all-rounder. Implies power,
decisiveness and technique
and, most importantly, the
ball not bouncing back out
of the net like it always used
to at the Dell. Perhaps that's
why Southampton built a
new stadium.

56. Squeezed

Requires slightly more finesse on the part of the goalscorer than its *scrambled* and *bundled* cousins.

57. Slid

Another type of goal that tends to go *home* rather than merely 'in'.

58. Floated

Rarely by design, floated free kicks (intended as a cross) can *evade everyone* in the box and *nestle* in the far corner. If it's your team conceding, you'll have spotted this depressing eventuality before the ball even entered the penalty area.

59. Sailed

More deliberate than *floating*, and more tranquil a goalscoring method than many above. Usually achieved from free kicks.

60. Screamer

What the kids are calling a *golazo* these days. Imagine the Twitter reaction to Ronnie Radford's epic effort in 1972.

61. Hooked

A fully paid-up volley, but one with more emphasis on technique than power and usually performed on the turn.

62. Acrobatic volley

As if bicycle kicks are some sort of forbidden brand name, or perhaps an exotic foreign-born luxury, some commentators prefer to call them *acrobatic volleys*.

63. Dipping volley

Aesthetically pleasing, even more so if it catches the crossbar on the way in.

64. Flying volley

Less spectacular than the *acrobatic* variety, but deserving of its own entry nevertheless.

65. Clipped

A deliberately subtle or deft touch to a teasing cross or, alternatively, a free kick delivered with excruciating precision – think Ronald Koeman against England in Rotterdam, 1993.

66. Trickled

That heartbreaking way that a ball crosses the line after a *defensive mix-up* between a *hapless* goalkeeper and one of his *Keystone Cops* defenders.

67. The slightest of touches

At first, easily mistaken as a free kick that has found its own way into the net. On closer inspection, *the slightest* (or *faintest*) *of touches* is all that was needed for a player to claim it.

68. Tucked

As tidy as it suggests, often finding its way under the goalkeeper's dive. A bit like *rifling*, perhaps, but with a silencer attached.

69. Clinical finish

Popularised by boyish-faced England *hitman* Gary Lineker in the mid-eighties. Less stylish than a goal scored with *aplomb*, but with noticeably more power.

70. Walking it in

This very rarely materialises, but is frequently threatened by teams claimed by the co-commentator to be *guilty of perhaps trying to walk the ball in at times*. Or, to give them their proper name, Arsenal.

71. Cross-cum-shot

Sometimes the dubious phenomenon of being *caught in two minds* can pay off. Goalkeepers can be left *red-faced* by a convenient *cross-cum-shot*, after which the inquest begins over whether the goalscorer meant it or not.

72. Rolled (into an empty net)

Unlike the *tap-in*, which is *put on a plate*, some easy finishes demand some hard work to enable them, such as rounding the goalkeeper first.

73. Sucked the ball in

This act of external assistance only happens at Anfield's Kop end, apparently, and probably only on its *special European nights*.

(Or Not)

74. Blazed

The most spectacular way to miss a chance, assuming the ball is sent as high over the crossbar as possible. *Clipping* or *shaving* the bar is never quite as emphatic.

75. Skied

Not particularly cryptic, even if the ball doesn't literally reach the sky – although we are all obliged to joke about the ball being *in orbit* or, at least, eventually landing in another postcode. If a gargantuan modern stadium renders the sky unattainable, *Row Z* is considered an acceptable substitute. Otherwise, there's...

76. Spooned

A more comical take on clearing the crossbar, often explained by our expert co-commentator as a result of *just leaning back a bit.*

77. Ballooned

A highly amusing way of missing the target – as its rather fun name suggests – reserved for overzealous penalty-taking and inexplicable blunders from extreme close-range.

78. Screwed

Taking one's eye off the ball can lead to this, as the ball skims off in the opposite direction to the intended target.

79. Sliced

Slicing a shot so badly that it might even go out for a throw-in is one of the most undignified potential pitfalls of attempted goalscoring, to the delighted reaction of the opposition supporters.[1]

80. Dragged

The opposite of screwed, as the ball is carelessly forced wide of the far post in a failed attempt at *burying*.

81. Crashed (against the woodwork)

Usually against the crossbar, after which the co-commentator is placed on Crossbarwatch, soon informing us that it is 'still shaking'.

82. Cannoned

Yet more old-fashioned firearms-based imagery, for when the ball rebounds off the woodwork (specifically the post, in this case) or another player.

83. The ball is in the net

Not strictly a miss, but if 'the ball is in the net' there's a fair chance the goal has, in fact, been disallowed. A common dramatic tool on *Soccer Saturday* or *Final Score*, to the point where surely nobody is in suspense any more.

84. If anything, almost hit too well

A highly complex phenomenon.[2]

---

1. See Chapter 12 for more on this phenomenon. **2.** 'If anything, Clive, he's almost hit that *too* well.' Many have pondered what this convoluted phrase actually means. Football has always had a problem with upper limits (the frequent demand for 'giving 110%', for example) but how can a shot be struck *too* well? The 'if anything' and 'almost' portions of this logic-defying observation suggest an inherent lack of faith in the whole concept. However, the generally accepted understanding is that it constitutes a shot that has been hit so powerfully that its impressive trajectory takes it narrowly high or wide of the goal.

85. Fluffed his lines

Football is a pantomime at the best of times, so occasionally a *big-money flop* can *fluff his lines* from close range. Strikers returning to their *old stomping ground* will resolutely stick to the proverbial *script*, but a surprise goalscorer may well deviate from it.

86. Squandered

The only things in life that can be *squandered* are money and goalscoring *opportunities*. Both can prove *costly* and may well be *rued*. *Squandered* also sounds more desperate than merely...

87. Wasted

88. Denied by the woodwork

Players and managers are keen to find any excuse for failure, but this act of conspiratorial anthropomorphism is a step too far. The goalposts don't move, after all.

89. When it seemed easier to score

A damning indictment of missing an open, or even *gaping*, goal.

90. My grandmother could have scored that

The relative of incredulous choice when voicing one's disapproval at a striker who fluffs the easiest of lines.

91. Sitter

Supposedly originating from game-shooting (i.e. a sitting target), this is the most traditional way to describe a simple but *squandered* goalscoring chance.

92. Saw the headlines

Very feasible. In the age of *muted celebrations* and pointing to the name on the back of their shirts, footballers are hyper-aware of their media coverage and this can lead to mid-game distraction.

93. Wild

An attempt at *thundering, hammering* or *lashing* which ends in total failure. A series of *wild* finishes runs the risk of being labelled...

94. Erratic

Certainly not the characteristic of a *natural finisher*, and implies that (as Glenn Hoddle once reportedly remarked of Andy Cole) a player may need several chances to score a goal.

95. Snatched at it

Fresh-faced, eager youngsters – even those hailed as *wonderkids* or *starlets* – are prone to *snatching at* chances, possibly with one eye on the potential headlines. Unless they happen to have an *old head on young shoulders*.

96. Caught in two minds

Unless it results in a goal from a *cross-cum-shot*, indecisiveness is never a good thing in front of goal. A rather hasty assumption for co-commentators to make, though – sometimes shots are so bad they simply look like aborted crosses, and vice versa.

97. Went for power over placement

Related to, if anything, *hitting the ball almost too well*. Opting for *power over placement* often results in merely *stinging the palms* of the goalkeeper.

98. Gilt-edged

Understandably, some people interpret this in commentary as 'guilt-edged', which would only further compound the misser's misery. *Gilt-edged* or *golden* chances are only ever deemed to be so when they are missed – no one has ever successfully converted a *gilt-edged* opportunity.

99. Tame effort

Lacking in power, even when some was intended. Can lead to *howls of derision* from the fans if the chance is particularly *gilt-edged*.

100. Scuffed

Hitting the ball into the ground, but not in a manner conducive to *slamming* and at the expense of power and direction. A common bedfellow of *snatching* at a chance.

101. Air-shot

The most humiliating of all misses, defying as it does the very literal point of 'football'. Likely to *sum up* a performance from a striker *devoid of confidence*.[3]

---

3. Confidence is one of two qualities of which footballers can be *devoid*, along with ideas.

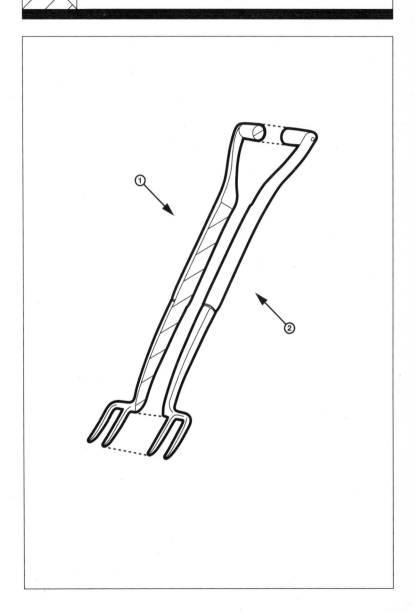

greasy
/griːsi/

adjective
1. covered with, resembling, or produced by grease or oil.

2. well-watered and conducive to getting the ball down and playing, albeit with the occasional loss of footing.

2. Every Blade of Grass: Navigating the Modern Football Pitch

Look up a World Cup final from the mid-twentieth century on YouTube and you'll notice very quickly just how slow football used to be. Any hint of panic would instantly be remedied with a prod of the ball back into the safe hands of the goalkeeper, who would punt the ball downfield at his leisure towards a lumbering No. 9 – a *traditional, genuine* one, of course, rather than the modern, *false* variety.

Then, in 1992, football's Big Bang occurred. A dull, cynical World Cup in Italy two years earlier had produced an average of 2.21 goals a game – which remains the lowest in the tournament's history – culminating in a dreadful final between West Germany and Argentina. Football's lawmakers began to brainstorm. It would be fascinating to discover the ideas of the International Football Association Board that never made it as far as the pitch, but the result of this enforced introspection was the single most important development in modern football history: the backpass rule. Outlawing the handling of a deliberate pass to the goalkeeper made with the boot (amended in 1997 to include throw-ins), the new directive transformed the dynamic of matches almost overnight, and followed the claim by FIFA's then general secretary, Sepp Blatter, that 'spectators do not go to football matches simply to see the goalkeeper standing still with the ball in his hands'.

Over two decades later, the game is – with a few notably diminutive exceptions – overrun by players built like super middleweight boxers, possessing the pace of 100-metre Olympians and breathing with the respiratory capacity of a varsity rowing crew. The Premier League's disputed credentials as the most exciting league in the world rely heavily on its characteristic *tempo*. Every frenetic, high-scoring match is billed as *a great advert* for the English top flight's brand.

In spite of Britain's footballing Age of Enlightenment, ushered in by envious glances towards Spain's assured major-tournament success, there remains in this country a visceral fascination with players who can run very quickly. For all the appreciation of skill and metronomic possession-hoarding, football is still a sucker for *pace* in any form – *searing, lightning, blistering* and *explosive pace* (often *to burn*); *bags of pace* or *pace in abundance*; and the curious concepts of *real* or *genuine pace*, suggesting that some players might be carrying counterfeit (or perhaps *deceptive*) *pace*. Speed appears to be everything; space is *burst into*, through-balls are *latched on to* and backpasses are *pounced on*. Insipid games, conspicuous by their lack of dynamism, require pace to be *injected* into them, something that has so far escaped the suspicious eye of sport's doping authorities. The hit is immediate and can be fleeting. Maximum velocity is surely achieved with that little sprint that substitutes break into as they *enter the fray*.

For all these descriptive terms to account for high-speed action, the other end of the scale is dealt with rather more tentatively. Forward players with great skill but who aren't blessed with speed – Dimitar Berbatov, for example – are viewed with suspicion, leading to the unhelpful labels of *enigmatic* and *mercurial*, and are frequently deemed to be lazy, *luxury players*. Footballers are rarely indicted outright as slow, but rather as *not the quickest* or perhaps *lacking that half a yard*. Injury can also rob a player of *that half a yard* or, in severe cases such as Fernando Torres, a full yard. This can prove problematic when they find themselves in a *footrace*, an oddly common turn of phrase which recalls the short-lived spectacle of the Rumbelows Sprint Challenge, held at Wembley in 1992 and never repeated. Such renowned speed merchants as Adrian Littlejohn of Sheffield United, Bournemouth's Efan Ekoku and Reading winger Michael Gilkes lined up in their football boots to charge down *the hallowed turf*, but it was Swansea's former Royal Mail worker John Williams who took the £10,000 prize and the nickname of 'The Flying Postman'.

It's not all high-velocity stuff, however. *Trudging* (sometimes *unrepentantly* so) is a common exit strategy of choice for red-carded players, while *nosebleed*-defying centre-halves tend to *amble forward* for set-pieces. An injured player's movement is always closely monitored by TV co-commentators, who keep us updated on his freedom of movement on a scale ranging from '*gingerly*' to '*moving a bit more freely now*'. Comfortable victories are made to sound leisurely, as the victors *stroll* or *cruise* past their hapless victims, without even getting *out of second gear*.

Beyond the mandatory dimensions of its playing area, football is subject to a set of curious, vague and often hyperbolic units of measurement. A player may find himself in *acres of space*, with *all the time in the world*, only to miss the goal by *a whisker* (or a *coat of paint*). Long-range shots (particularly *speculative* efforts from players *trying their luck*) are attempted from *all of* thirty-five yards, while aggressors run *fully fifty yards to get involved* in a melee – an act always deemed highly unnecessary by the onlooking co-commentator – and the same guesstimated distance is usually achieved with a *raking pass*. Offside decisions are knee-jerkingly appraised against the wildly disparate benchmarks of *half a yard* or *miles* on or off, as if anything in between is just too mundane for words.

Modern footballers must know their place, even if most of them are helpless chess pieces moved around at will by their gesticulating manager. But, while the positions they are allocated have well-established names, the areas of the pitch they occupy are still subject to the eccentricity of the football cliché.

The engine room

Smack-bang in the *middle of the park* is the British Crown dependency of the midfield *engine room*, traditionally the domain of the Lampards and the Gerrards *of this world*. As the name suggests, every player operating within this industrial environment must possess a *great engine*, or at least be *full of running*. The engine room is governed by *midfield generals*, who patrol the area while clutching the *scruff of the* game's *neck* and issuing the occasional *licence to get forward* to their more attack-minded colleagues.

Space is at a premium here, but the engine room must accommodate a whole range of players. *Tigerish* midfielders *scuttle* and *scurry* in their fight to earn, oddly, *the lion's share of possession*. Graceful playmakers are said to *glide across the turf*, while their more energetic team-mates find themselves making *lung-bursting runs* upfield, after which they must still *bust a gut* to get into the penalty area. *Mazy runs* are almost always *embarked on*, for some reason.

There's so much going on in the average *engine room* that it's no wonder it's so often cited as where a game *will be won or lost*.

The hole

The hole is fast becoming a quaint anachronism in an era where the unsophisticated 4-4-2 exists merely to be infiltrated, between its lines, by interchanging attackers. Old-fashioned centre-halves, hoping for a ding-dong battle with an equally old-fashioned centre-forward, find themselves befuddled with no one to mark. *The hole* is the place in which to *slalom*, *waltz*, *probe* and *scheme* in between the opponents' *two banks of four*.

Wide areas

The increasing obsolescence of the chalk-booted, *jinking*, out-and-out winger has rendered their natural habitat redefined as the more vague-sounding *wide areas*. The wide areas are where these *jet-heeled tormentors-in-chief* aim to give opposing full-backs as *torrid a time* as possible.

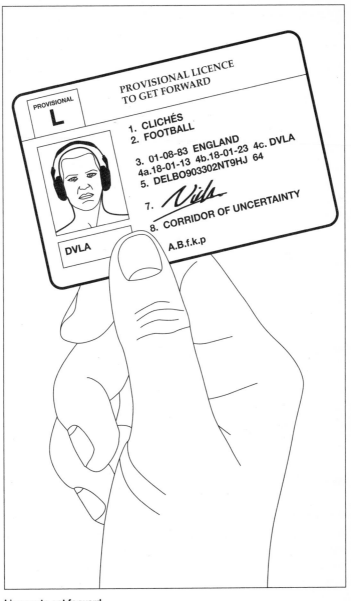

PROVISIONAL LICENCE TO GET FORWARD

PROVISIONAL
L

1. CLICHÉS
2. FOOTBALL
3. 01-08-83 ENGLAND
4a.18-01-13 4b.18-01-23 4c. DVLA
5. DELBO903302NT9HJ 64
7. *Nick*
8. CORRIDOR OF UNCERTAINTY

DVLA

A.B.f.k.p

Licence to get forward

They may find, however, that their adversary is *no slouch* and he himself may *need no invitation* to *bomb on*. The historically undersung full-back has gradually been liberated by the era of relative gung ho-ism that the backpass rule ushered in. They are now free to *buccaneer* or *maraud* to their lungs' content, provided they are just as good *going the other way*.

The wide areas are where teams are most likely to find *all kinds of space*, or even *oceans of room* from which to generate *wave after wave of attacks*. Their opponents may be able to *keep them at bay* – unless their defence is *all at sea* – but it certainly requires *all hands to the pump*.

Going nowhere

It is usually here where a bumbling winger, in a desperate attempt to track back, fouls an opponent as they loiter (going the wrong way) in this particularly innocuous part of the pitch. Located near half-way and close to the touchline, the vast majority of free kicks conceded here will be classified as *needless* or *silly*. Such is the desolation in this area of the pitch that it can be the only logical setting for the proverbial *periphery of the game*, to which ineffective, *enigmatic* players are often forced, to such an extent that they *go missing*.

The channels

The thinking-man's wings, the channels represent the dire straits between penalty area and touchline where *swashbuckling* wide men claim their bounty. The most honest and underappreciated footballer, the *willing runner*, is also put to work in the channels, *ploughing a lone furrow*. Should his perseverance fail to pay off or his endeavour go without reward, he may begin to *cut a forlorn figure* up front. The channels can be particularly wasteful places,

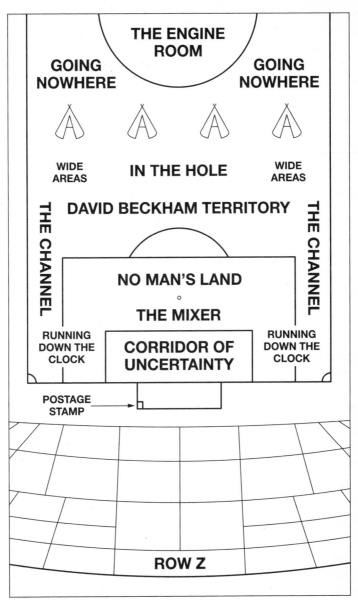

Mapping the pitch

characterised by overhit passes which *ask too much of* their intended recipient, who – as the commentator will confirm – is 'quick but he's not *that* quick!'

David Beckham territory

An area of hotly disputed sovereignty, but various attempts to annex it permanently over the last decade have proved fruitless, many coming to an ignominious end up in *Row Z*. If a dead-ball specialist is to claim the territory for himself now Beckham has hung up his boots, he must first *pull rank*.

It is the most popular strategic base to launch attacks on the tiny enclave in the top corner of the goal – known as the *postage stamp* – located just next to the *angle of post and bar*.

The mixer

The great leveller. From Sunday league to the top flight, a *last throw of the dice* is punted hopefully into this most chaotic of last-chance saloons, where reputations and price tags are rarely respected. Inside *the mixer* lie discarded, rusting *kitchen sinks* from previous acts of attacking desperation by teams who had long since been *camped in the opposition half. The mixer* is located in the heart of the opponents' penalty area, which is itself a sub-district of *the final third*, in which the *end product* is paramount and the nebulous concept of *quality* (even *just that little bit of quality*) is notably lacking.

No man's land

A horrid void in which hapless goalkeepers are prone to *going walkabout* in an attempt to rescue a *suicidal backpass* from well outside their comfort zone. Poor goalkeepers have suffered more than most from the relentless post-1992 tempo, and must now *earn their corn* by *backpedalling*, *onrushing*, *charging out* and *scrambling* their way around the markedly less safe confines of their penalty area.

The corridor of uncertainty

One of the most poetic of all the football clichés. Originally a cricket phrase, but now undeniably adopted by football. The narrow *corridor of uncertainty* straddles the six-yard line, and is permeated regularly by crosses *fizzed in* from *the channels*.

It also provides the acid test for the confidence of a striker, and whether he is prepared to *gamble* on a cross into this dangerous area, be it via *darting* into the near post, or by *ghosting in* at the *back stick*.

3. The Goalkeepers' Union

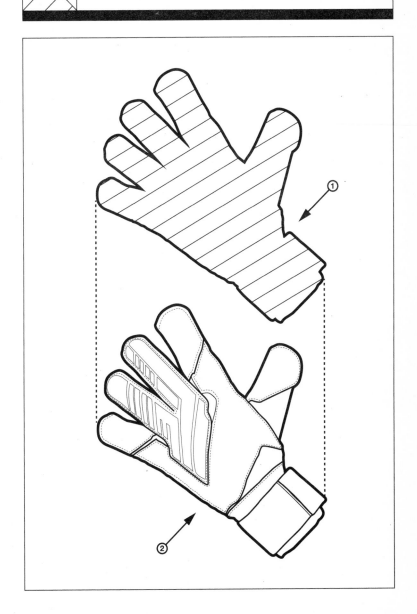

elect
/ɪˈlɛkt/

verb

1. choose (someone) to hold public office or some other position by voting.

2. choose, as a goalkeeper, to punch the ball clear instead of catching it (much to UK-based disapproval).

3. The Goalkeepers' Union

Football's constant wish to transcend itself is perhaps best demonstrated by the hypermythology of The Goalkeeper. Crazy, mad, lonely, *different*. Unfortunately for this existential narrative, for every Albert Camus or René Higuita there is a Chris Kirkland or a Richard Wright.

However, for all the tactical tinkering of the last 150 years, the lone responsibility of the goalkeeper has remained intact and distinct from the ball-playing chess pieces in front of them. In that time, keepers have established a hefty sub-genre of football clichés that both legitimises and undermines the unique experience of being between the sticks. The *Goalkeepers' Union* remains the busiest fictional trade union in the world, convening regularly to renegotiate their traditional overprotection or to discuss their collective reaction to the new World Cup match ball. David 'Calamity' James (now retired but fighting the cause from his punditry position) is perhaps its incumbent general secretary, with his imaginary desk boasting a 'You don't have to be mad to work here, but it helps!!!' sign.

It's certainly a brave man that *plies his trade* as the most frequently exposed player on the pitch. There are no hiding places for goalkeepers and, such is the loneliness that supposedly plagues No.1s, they often resort to *wishing the ground would open up and swallow them*. As well as the seemingly future-proof chant of 'Yyyyyou're-shit-AAAAaahhhh!' that soundtracks every goal-kick, their isolation is charmingly illustrated by a tale from Huddersfield Town's fondly remembered 'Cowshed' terrace at their old Leeds Road ground. As the visiting goalkeeper trotted over to take his place for kick-off, the boisterous home contingent would sportingly applaud him. On the cue of his raising of an appreciative glove, the Cowshed would then suddenly show their true colours by hurling abuse and mockery at the cruelly hoodwinked soul.

The equally merciless caricature of the goalkeeper as a hapless bumbler can also be traced back to its roots. Polish goalkeeper Jan Tomaszewski, whose array of acrobatics at Wembley in 1973 meant England missed out on the World Cup the following year, was described before the game as a 'circus clown in gloves' by Brian Clough. But do clowns theoretically make bad goalkeepers? Despite being prone to the occasional high-profile gaffe, they remain comfortable performing in front of huge crowds, possess established ball-handling skills and are the very embodiment of the *unorthodox-but-effective* approach.

Apart from the significant inconvenience of being forbidden from handling backpasses since 1992, the role of the goalkeeper has had little opportunity for evolution. Even the name for their position scarcely has room for nuance. While the contracted term of *keeper* has made a comfortable bed for itself in the football language – shedding its superfluous apostrophe in the process – its erstwhile rival abbreviation of *goalie* has seemingly gone the way of Ceefax and affordable ticket prices (for reasons not quite clear) and faded from view. This leaves that most awkward and contrived of footballing synonyms, *custodian*, which won't be embraced in this chapter or any other of this book. As defenders, midfielders and attackers continue to reinvent themselves and blur the tactical boundaries, the goalkeeper can only remain a goalkeeper. Any Sunday league player-manager can testify to the fruitless weekly search for a willing *custodian* (damn, there it is), such is the limited appeal of endlessly fetching the ball from a hedgerow before taking a goal-kick in horizontal rain.

Thankfully, though, there are some eccentrics still willing to go between the sticks. To keep these unpredictable scatterbrains on the straight and narrow, a set of failsafe commandments exists.

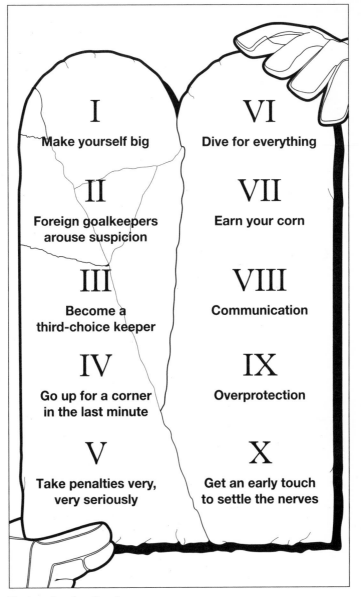

The ten rules of goalkeeping

The Ten Rules of Goalkeeping

1. Make yourself big

A method pioneered (albeit in its literal sense) by William 'Fatty' Foulke at the end of the nineteenth century, mastered by Neville Southall in the 1980s, and made popular by Peter Schmeichel in the nineties, *making yourself big* is not a complicated concept. By increasing their surface area, an onrushing goalkeeper can minimise the likelihood of the ball going past, thereby *thwarting* the opposing striker.

2. Foreign goalkeepers arouse suspicion

'He doesn't fancy it, does he?'
The well-documented *foreign influx* to the Premier League brought with it a unique breed of goalkeeper. They wore tracksuit bottoms. They dared to bare their forearms. They were even comfortable with the ball at their feet, the bastards. But put them under a high ball, co-commentators assured us, and they'd fall apart within minutes. If they didn't *flap* at a cross, they'd certainly *elect to punch* the ball away instead of risking physical contact by trying to catch it.

Then, as English football *stopped producing goalkeepers in the same numbers any more*, we learned to stop worrying and love the Continental *custodians*. Now our homegrown keepers are also punching unconvincingly and refusing to take any chances with swerving pot-shots from distance.

3. Become a third-choice keeper

The third-choice goalkeeper faces a continuous battle with the fourth official over the dubious honour of having the easiest-looking job in football. In return for their seemingly comfortable existence, they rarely kick up a fuss about their limited playing time. They are the supply teachers of football, ready to pack up their belongings and turn up somewhere else on an emergency loan, their career trajectory dictated by the ominous *special dispensation.*

One rung up the pecking order, the substitute goalkeeper faces a more mentally taxing existence. One moment, they're tucked away on the bench, chewing gum and sharing an odd chuckle with a fellow sub. The next, they're pressed into action after an injury or a sending-off, the latter frequently thrusting them straight into the self-contained drama of a penalty kick. Will their *first task be to pick the ball out of the net?* Or will they be suddenly cast into the role of *instant hero?*

4. Go up for a corner in the last minute

A delightful phenomenon. His team are desperately chasing a goal and manage to win a corner deep into stoppage time.[1] Their goalkeeper consults the bench, as protocol demands, and is given the go-ahead to *venture* upfield. Before the eighty-eighth minute, he would be waved back, but this is most certainly *last-chance saloon.*

The incongruous sight of this towering, begloved presence in the penalty area sends all concerned into a state of emergency. For the defending side, an immediate quandary: who should be deployed to mark him? Is he as much of a goal threat as a 40-goal-a-season striker or an imposing centre-half? On the

1. Given the alarming frequency of last-minute corners awarded to teams who desperately require a goal, one wonders if supposedly impartial referees actually want to see a goalkeeper come up for a corner as much as the rest of us.

other hand, the corner-taker must decide if his *final throw of the dice* should be directly aimed at this *last-gasp* attacking charlatan.

To justify his gamble, the goalkeeper strains every sinew to reach the ball with his head, willed on not just by his own supporters but by every single neutral onlooker. Despite the occasional Jimmy Glass moment, a goal very rarely results. We are then treated to the bonus secondary spectacle of whether or not the defending team can take advantage of the unattended goal at the other end.

Novel moments of role reversal in football are a unifying delight. The opposite of a goalkeeper-turned-goalscorer is when an outfield player is forced to *don the gloves*. This represents the graduation *from bad to worse* for a team who are already several goals down with all three substitutions made. Once the semi-willing stand-in has stepped forward, the excited murmurs from the crowd begin as he awkwardly pulls on the ill-fitting goal-keeper shirt. Our excitement and curiosity are usually rewarded by a string of instinctive saves with his feet, punctuated by bouts of earnest motivational clapping towards his defenders.

5. Take penalties very, very seriously

The quickest route to goalkeeping heroism is through saving a penalty. Given the hopelessness of the situation – a highly skilled, specially selected player given the chance to shoot from twelve yards, in their own time, against an opponent who can't move from his line – you'd think keepers would be a little more happy if they win the duel. But the penalty-save 'celebration' is a peculiarly stern-faced affair. As the ball is cleared away, team-mates' gleeful advances are shoved away as they're furiously reminded of their duties – there are strikers to man-mark and a match to be won. Should the goalkeeper narrowly fail to save a penalty, as the ball *squirms* underneath him, it is the nearest goalpost that takes the brunt of his inevitable frustration.

6. Dive for everything

Shot-stopper has long been somewhat of a backhanded compliment for otherwise limited goalkeepers, but it remains the most eye-catching part of their repertoire. You never hear of a *statuesque* keeper making a save, whether the incoming shot is at *a good height for a goalkeepe*r (anywhere between the knee and the nipple) or *destined for the top corner* (a destiny that's never fulfilled).

Smart saves (also known as *smart stops* or *getting down smartly*) specifically take place low at the near post, at which a goalkeeper is inevitably deemed to be *disappointed* to concede[2] should the ball get past him. While outfield players keep certain elements of skill in their proverbial locker, a goalkeeper stores his most impressive shot-stopping in his *top drawer*. With his goal *under siege*, the keeper may find himself *clawing* or *beating* balls away while his goal *leads a charmed life*. For all his efforts, however, a goalkeeper can only ever be *equal to* anything that comes his way.

Double- or even triple-saves are overwhelmingly hailed as significantly greater than the sum of their average parts and, along with saving penalties, are the most effective way for a goalkeeper to get noticed. The odd unnecessarily acrobatic save – *one for the cameras* – along the way won't do any harm, either.

7. Earn your corn

While glamorous outfield players enjoy multimillion pound contracts, toiling goalkeepers are apparently paid in crop yields. Other foodstuffs are available, however, as incentives for routine achievements between the sticks: *bread-and-butter saves* are the sort you'd expect anybody to make; uncontested, lofted balls into the box constitute their *meat and drink* (more troublesome

---

2. '*Disappointed*' acts as a catch-all term for a range of footballing emotions, from mild regret to burning injustice.

crosses, however, arrive in the form of a *peach*); and shots hit directly at the goalkeeper, particularly with some force, simply go *straight down their throat*.

One of the *Goalkeepers' Union's* greatest accomplishments is to achieve an impressive shelf-life for its members. With keepers supposedly not peaking until their early thirties, and many comfortably competing at the top level into their fifth decade (providing they *look after themselves*), there is a great deal of *corn* to be *earned* in the average career.

8. Communication

Defenders frequently *need a shout*, if only to protect against *defensive mix-ups*. Bawling at a defence is a vital part of a goalkeeper *commanding his penalty area*; from the simple instructions (the ubiquitous and helpful shout of 'AWAY!' as a corner flies in) to the painstakingly precise construction of a defensive wall for a free kick, which requires the keeper to lean against his post and direct his defenders to the right or left, a few centimetres at a time.

One piece of goalkeeping code is yet to be cracked, however. The cryptic semaphore exchange between a corner-taker (one or two hands held aloft) and his opposing goalkeeper (two arms in the air) may well hold the answer to the meaning of life.

9. Overprotection

Goalkeepers are overprotected these days, as the average co-commentator likes to point out – with a hint of a sneer because, as an ex-pro whose playing days fell just before the Premier League jackpot era, it's his job to give us the dystopian bigger picture of ghastly modern football from time to time.

The mollycoddling of modern goalkeepers perhaps stems

from Nat Lofthouse's rather *agricultural* goal for Bolton Wanderers in the 1958 FA Cup final, where both the ball and Manchester United keeper Harry Gregg found themselves in the back of the Wembley net. Goalkeepers went on to become a protected species, while the *old-fashioned English No. 9s* barely survived beyond the Pathé newsreels.

10. Get an early touch to settle the nerves

All crises of confidence, afflicting either inexperienced or out-of-form goalkeepers, can apparently be resolved with an early touch of the ball, even a brief one with the feet. Perhaps this is why sympathetic referees, in accordance with their long-established policy of overprotection, are seen to let the goalkeepers give the match ball a good squeeze and a bounce in the tunnel before kick-off.

Even if an early, calming feel of the ball is secured, the goalkeeper's apparently fragile psyche can still be turned upside down by a period of relative inactivity. Should his side be in sufficient control of the game he may become a *virtual spectator* or *virtual bystander*, placing him in some sort of trance until he is finally *called upon* to make a save.

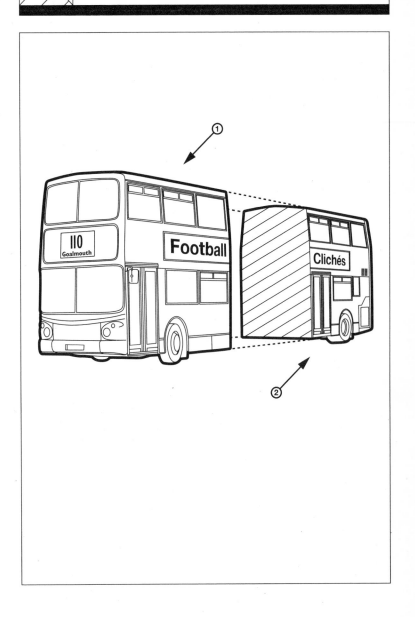

lynchpin
/lɪn(t)ʃpɪn/

noun

1. a pin passed through the end
of an axle to keep a wheel in position.

2. a long-serving (possibly *grizzled*)
centre-half, integral to a team's
back four.

4. The No-Nonsense Art of Defending

In a technical sense, at least, defenders are hugely unappreciated. There is an overwhelmingly physical emphasis on praising the *all-hands-to-the-pump* achievements of a *rearguard*, whose component parts are hailed as *immense*, a *colossus* or a *rock*.

Individual acclaim is traditionally thin on the ground for defenders. Of the fifty-eight Ballon d'Or winners to date, only three primarily *plied their trade* in their own half; Franz Beckenbauer (twice) and Matthias Sammer took full advantage of their eye-catching sweeper roles but only 2006 winner Fabio Cannavaro could be considered as an out-and-out defender. Standing a mere 5ft 9in (a sexier version of mid-nineties Wimbledon stopper Chris Perry, if you will), Cannavaro had to captain his country to World Cup glory before being considered for football's biggest individual prize.

Defenders are ultimately able to avenge this glaring lack of recognition by becoming managers and pundits. Having spent their careers watching much of the game unfold in front of them, they have arguably developed a greater appreciation of the collective means by which greedy strikers complete their glory-stealing end. The lengthy Monday night Sky Sports lectures from Gary Neville and fellow *student of the game* Jamie Carragher – the Ant and Dec of dour defending – are our plasma-screen punishment for habitually downplaying the complexity of keeping the ball out of your own net.

It seems more than mere coincidence that the most prominent analytical voices in football broadcasting belong to former defenders. Alan Hansen, who bowed out of *Match of the Day* duties after the World Cup in Brazil, was once peerless in his Saturday-night dissection of Premier League defending. Rarely one to overreact, Hansen could be trusted to provide a faithful account of a team's defending and his analysis – making

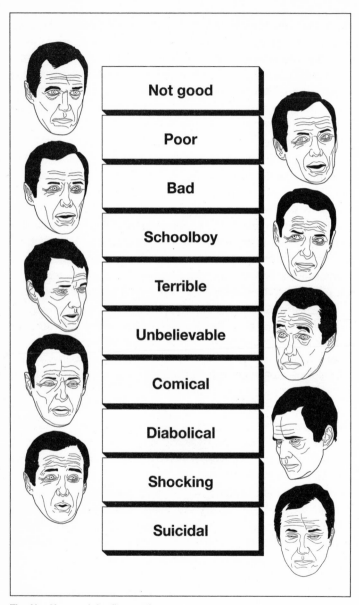

The Alan Hansen defending continuum

careful use of appropriate adjectives – formed the template with which all rearguards should be judged (see diagram on page 60).

Thanks to the forensic breaking-down of the finer points of a backline's duties, it has become clear just what constitutes good (or indeed bad) defending.

Sensing danger

One thing that defenders seem to do routinely, but which excites pundits immeasurably, is to *see the danger and deal with it*. 'Dealing with it' is allowed to consist of merely hoofing it into *Row Z*, as this is manfully regarded as *no-nonsense*. Whole *Match of the Day* montages can be formed from a cluster of rather straightforward interceptions, blocks and clearances, all rather greater than the sum of their parts. Danger can also be *smelt*, but its fragrance is yet to be widely documented.

Sensing danger is part of the wider defensive quality of being able to *read the game*. A useful tool for defenders who are *not the quickest*, reading the game is invariably traced back to Bobby Moore, one of the first players found to have the rather handy *first yard in his head*.

Switching off

As one of football's cardinal sins, especially at the top level, *switching off* is never a good idea. Many a goal has been caused by defenders not concentrating, and many risk being associated permanently with being *prone to lapses of concentration*. Quickly taken short corners have a particularly anaesthetising effect on opponents who, after having *gone to sleep*, are awoken only by the apoplectic clapping of their exposed goalkeeper.

Desperation

Some of football's most evocative language is reserved for moments of defensive emergency. The most heroic tackles, blocks and clearances are of the *last-ditch* variety but, among the blood and thunder, certain subtleties exist. Being *everywhere* is quite the opposite to being *all over the place*, while figurative *buses* are either *parked* by obdurate defences or driven through the middle of them. Most confusingly, the apparently opposite concepts of *setting your stall out* and *shutting up shop* actually mean the same thing when it comes to defensive strategy.

If being physically extended isn't enough, desperate defending is also mentally taxing. *Probing* forward lines seek to *ask questions* of a defence with the aim of posing them *all sorts of problems*. The most crucial period of interrogation is the all-important (yet arbitrarily established) opening twenty minutes, in which the underdog is obliged to *keep it tight*.

When this resistance is finally broken, *the floodgates* may then open, at which point it becomes an exercise of *damage limitation*.

Mix-ups

All defenders live in fear of the *defensive mix-up* but are resigned to its inevitability. Repeatedly co-starring the goalkeeper, *defensive mix-ups* can, at worst, leave the opposing striker with the *simple task of rolling the ball into the empty net*. The post-mortem of a *defensive mix-up* will likely conclude that the defender *needed a shout there*. Handily, and with glorious HD hindsight, the pundit will also point out that one of them *just needed to take charge and deal with it*.

The constant threat of a *defensive mix-up* may explain why, over twenty years after the backpass rule was introduced, a simple header back to the goalkeeper is still met with a ripple of applause. It's not appreciation, it's sheer relief.

Match of the Day editors have perfected the art of suspense in these situations. Just as alarm bells automatically start ringing if the highlights show a player picking up a booking, there's always something suspicious about a defence casually knocking the ball to each other. It's a little like the initially innocuous videos on *You've been Framed*; the camera lingers a little too long and it emerges that something is surely about to go catastrophically awry.

A momentary slip can befall even the best defenders, but extended periods of slapstick can result in a *comedy of errors* at the back, often charmingly based on early twentieth-century silent-film characters the *Keystone Cops*. An even older cultural reference that has survived the test of time is *at sixes and sevens*, the origin of which is disputable. Depending on who you believe, it derives either from a Chaucerian phrase from the mid-1380s, relating to a two-dice game called 'Hazard', or a long-running dispute between two London livery companies in the fifteenth century over their position in the order of precedence. Either way, it has survived for centuries to become the standard description for a moment of costly disorganisation at the heart of a back four.

Fear of pace

Defenders don't like playing against pace. In fact, as Alan Hansen very possibly has tattooed somewhere on his body, *if there's one thing defenders hate, it's pace*. It terrifies them. Pace can be used to give them *a torrid time, roast* them, *turn them inside out, expose* them or *destroy* them.

Marking

A close-quarters task, requiring the defender to be all over his opponent *like a rash*, thereby *not giving him a sniff*. *Enigmatic* players, said to *go missing in big games*, may eventually be found languishing in their adversary's *pocket*, much to the satisfaction and amusement of opposing fans.

Claudio Gentile's ninety-minute slow torture of Diego Maradona at the 1982 World Cup remains the all-time hatchet-man masterpiece. Gentile fouled his target, on average, every four minutes as Italy marched on to the final. Not since has a *danger man* been so brutally *shackled*.

Tackling

Modern-day defenders cannot get away with the bone-crunching tackles of yesteryear. Any challenge that falls into the *agricultural* bracket should be met with at least a caution but, in some sort of tackling revolution, these seem to be giving way to *industrial* challenges. In these stricter times, defenders must learn to stay on their feet and not *commit themselves* by *going to ground*. Flying wingers can be frustrated by defenders *shepherding* the ball over the touchline, the only act of *shepherding* in life that takes place in the absence of any sheep.

An eye-catching tackle is the most visceral string to a defender's bow. A well-timed slide challenge (ideally one that hooks the ball neatly away from the tumbling victim) is a guaranteed crowd-pleaser, as is the unique, booming '*ger-dung*' sound of a perfectly balanced, full-blooded block tackle.

Much like when defenders suffer the proverbial *nosebleed* when he pops up in the opponents' penalty area, attackers are rarely welcome in their own box for fear of committing a *forward's challenge* and giving away a cheap penalty. When the situation demands it, though, a spot of tracking back from a striker is more likely to get them into their defenders' good books.

The demands on the undervalued modern defender are huge. Simultaneously, he must have his opponent *in his pocket* while maintaining his concentration and reading the danger, while *leaping prodigiously* and doing *just enough*, while being comfortable on the ball and making a *last-ditch* tackle. All with his *body on the line* and *all hands to the pump*.

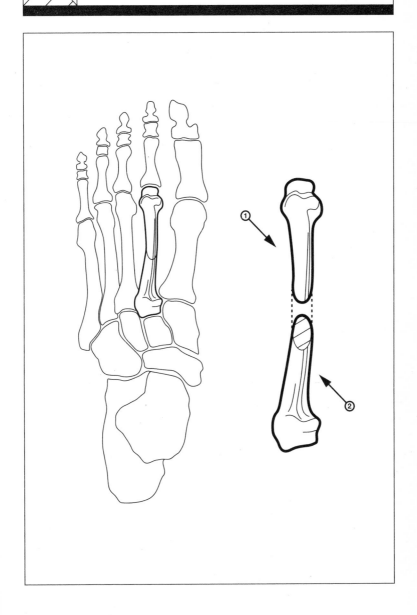

innocuous
/ɪˈnɒkjʊəs/

adjective
1. not harmful or offensive.

2. An injury sustained with no other player *within yards of the victim.*

5. The Anatomy of a Footballer

Professional footballers are apparently not built like you and I and it certainly isn't just about their feet. From head to toe, their bodies are subject to an entirely different terminology to the Average Joe.

A footballer's head is equally important in a figurative sense as in a physical one. Notably composed youngsters are said to have an *old head on young shoulders*, at least until they *lose their head*, at which point they may well need *an arm around their shoulder*. Should an in-form player *have his head turned* by interest from a bigger club, he may find himself ruled out of contention for the next match because his *head's not right*, although this may actually help to soothe his manager's *selection headache*. Should his dream move not materialise, the player is best advised to *get his head down* (as well as *knuckling down*) and work hard in training.

A predatory striker is said to have an *eye for goal*, which occasionally involves *giving the goalkeeper the eyes* (having seen *the whites* of them), despite often having *one eye* (or *half an eye*) *on* an upcoming fixture. Key players in big matches are likely to have *all eyes on* them, even if they're secretly *eyeing a move* to a side whose football is more *easy on the eye*. Meanwhile, today's mutant referees are required to have *eyes in the back of their head*, lagging behind their highly evolved *eagle-eyed* assistants. Calling upon the other senses, players can *sniff out a chance* if their team *smells blood* (unless they're *not given a sniff*) but only after the two teams have finished *feeling each other out*.

A goalkeeper faces the frequent prospect of a shot arriving *straight down his throat*, which is much less threatening in reality and simply ends up in his *grateful hands*. Necks are where *big-money signings* must wear their *price tags*, while a game's neck must have its proverbial *scruff* taken by an engine-room midfielder.

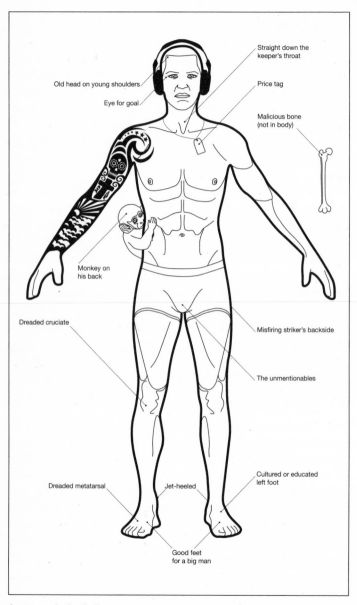

Anatomy of a footballer

A particularly *goal-shy* centre-forward must bear the burden of both *a monkey* and *the crowd on his back*, in addition to his hefty price tag. The well-established remedy for his goal drought, however, is for *one to go in off his backside*. No sports scientist has yet been able to determine the whereabouts of a player's *engine*, but it is likely to be found in a *lung-bursting* location near the centre of the body. There's no real room for innuendo in football commentary, but a great deal of mirth is reserved for when a player is struck in the *unmentionables* by a shot or a boot.

Unsurprisingly for outfield players, hands and arms are a consistently controversial region of the body. Penalty areas are serial witnesses to a *suspicion of a hand*, while everyone knows that *as soon as you raise your hands, you're asking for trouble*. Goalkeepers, meanwhile, must possess a *strong hand* while making sure errant crosses are *plucked out of the air* using their *grateful hands*. Their *palms*, however, exist only to be *stung*.

And so the business end of the footballer's anatomy. The legs seem the most obvious place to find the ever-elusive *malicious bone*, but loyal managers continue to refute its existence in their players' bodies. When a footballer finally loses *that half a yard*, it is said that his *legs have gone*. Luckily, *fresh legs* are always on hand (so to speak) to replace them.

Understandably, the lower extremities are subject to the most well-worn clichés. *Flat-footed* defenders are exposed by *fleet-footed* wingers, and *run ragged* by *jet-heeled* ones. There is a long-established bias towards the exotic, sinistral footballer – left feet are *educated* and *cultured* magic *wands* that can *open a tin of beans*, while any old neanderthal can swing his right boot. Cautionary tales of footballers who fall from grace often lament how they *had the world at their feet*. Collectively speaking, whole teams can have *one foot in the final* (assuming they have the opposition on *the back foot*), in which they may find themselves with *one hand on the trophy*.

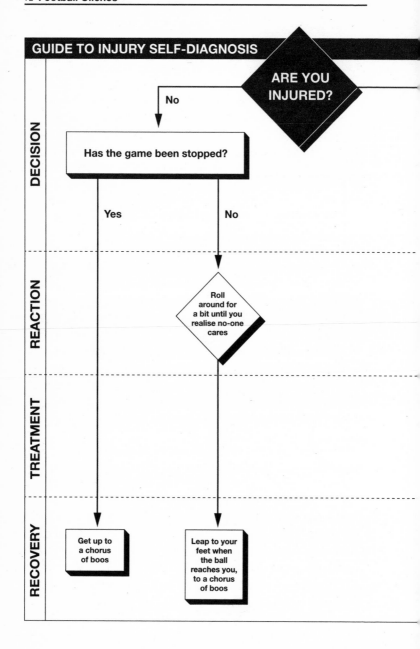

GUIDE TO INJURY SELF-DIAGNOSIS

ARE YOU INJURED?

No

DECISION

Has the game been stopped?

Yes   No

REACTION

Roll around for a bit until you realise no-one cares

TREATMENT

RECOVERY

Get up to a chorus of boos

Leap to your feet when the ball reaches you, to a chorus of boos

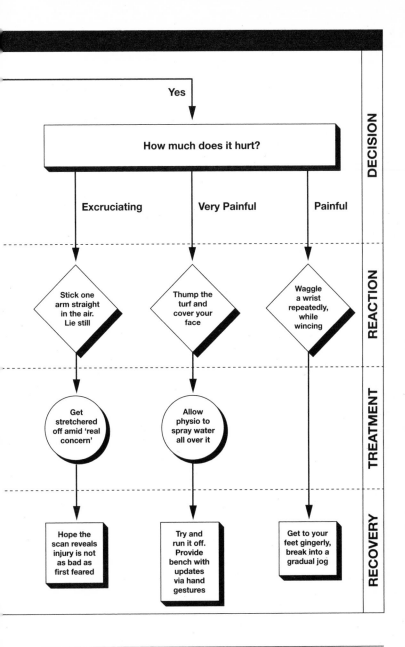

Yes

DECISION

How much does it hurt?

Excruciating   Very Painful   Painful

REACTION

Stick one arm straight in the air. Lie still

Thump the turf and cover your face

Waggle a wrist repeatedly, while wincing

TREATMENT

Get stretchered off amid 'real concern'

Allow physio to spray water all over it

RECOVERY

Hope the scan reveals injury is not as bad as first feared

Try and run it off. Provide bench with updates via hand gestures

Get to your feet gingerly, break into a gradual jog

The most notable part of the lower-body skeleton is surely *the dreaded metatarsal*, which humans only developed in the early 2000s if the succession of major tournament-disrupting breaks to various key England players are anything to go by.

Despite the purists' protestations that football is becoming a non-contact sport, the unique anatomy of its finely tuned athletes is at constant risk of strain, crack and rupture. Injury news struggles to fill the void created by the *slamming shut* of the transfer window but, in between matches, the reliable conveyor belt of *knocks*, *problems* and *strains* provides some grist for the media mill. With injuries long accepted as *part and parcel of the game*, the media are equally as prepared for them as the clubs' medical teams.

Broadly speaking, injury news is delivered in two forms: *boosts* and *blows*. An *injury boost* usually involves a player returning to fitness ahead of schedule or discovering that an injury is *not as bad as first feared*. When long-term absentees are finally given the go-ahead for a return to action, after coming through a behind-closed-doors friendly *unscathed*, their amnesiac managers consider them as *almost like a new signing*.

On the other hand, *injury blows* can strike at the most inconvenient moment, throwing preparations into chaos and *derailing* title challenges. Thanks in part to the *Football Manager* series of computer games, we simply must know the prognosis of a footballer's injury, with a return date accurate to days and weeks. Managers find themselves being asked for timeframes for recovery straight after the matches, but we are urged to wait for the results of the omniscient *scan*, on which everyone involved will be said to *sweat*. Intrepid journalists, meanwhile, prepare us for the worst by reporting that the player in question 'left the stadium on crutches'.

Injuries suffered before particularly important matches can set up a dramatic *race to be fit*, which must be clarified further as being *against time*, just in case anyone mistakenly believes that several crocked team-mates are gorging on horse placenta in oxygen tents to see who can get back on the pitch first. Again, the modern demand for quantifying a player's fitness progress leads to managers being asked to rate, as a percentage, their ailing star's chances of making the squad. A simple but tantalising '50-50' response is usually enough for the match preview writers, and keeps the race to be fit going all the way to the wire (or, at least, a last-minute fitness test on the pitch).

Gambling on a player's dubious *touch-and-go* fitness can backfire, with various onlookers using their 20-20 hindsight to declare that he was *patently unfit*. Despite advances in injury prevention and treatment, the best measure is still accepted to be *wrapping the player in cotton wool*.

Niche categories of injury include the *innocuous* injury, characteristically sustained when there's no one near the victim and which tends to be quite serious. Lightening the mood is the more amusing *freak injury*, which has inextricably linked Dave Beasant and salad cream for all eternity.

A trickier part of the co-commentator's remit is to provide rudimentary medical reports whenever a player goes down with an injury, confirming what our own eyes have told us by observing that a player may have *fallen a bit awkwardly there* but with the added insight that *he'll run that off*. But it's the co-commentator's after-care that really stands out: while the game goes on, he is able to give us live updates on how freely the victim is now moving, how happy he looks (often *not happy at all*) and, in more severe cases, whether his *afternoon/evening is over*.

Clashes of heads are mostly *sickening*, and the sight of any blood will lead Dr Co-Commentator to diagnose it as *a nasty one.* The silver lining, though, is that an eye-catching head bandage is as cast-iron a guarantee of the three points/ qualification/cup final victory as it's possible to secure. Games can be *marred* by a *horror injury*; more specifically, wins are *overshadowed* (or at least have their *gloss* taken off) and the misery of defeat is somewhat *compounded.*

In the longer term, luckless players can find their careers *plagued* or, worse, *ravaged* by a *catalogue of injuries*. Countless *setbacks* may finally force a player to *hang up his boots*, lest his failing body deny him the chance *to play football in the garden with his kids*. Curiously, a player's *injury hell* or *injury nightmare* is usually only defined once he has finally returned to action. Whole clubs are equally at risk of being defined by a perennial *injury crisis* that *decimates* their squad and keeps the *treatment table* in constant use. Squad-wide injuries tend to come in a *spate* which, in turn, can lead to a *raft of withdrawals* from the increasingly unattractive chore of international duty.

There is a disproportionate fascination with players returning from injury wearing some extra protection. Paul Gascoigne was a trendsetter back in 1993 with his *protective* mask (always a protective mask, lest anyone think these players might have been making some sort of fashion statement) and the fixation has continued to the present day with Petr Cech's rugby cap.

With televised football, and more recently the player-cam innovation, players are under constant scrutiny. Commentators and TV directors have developed a keen eye for the body language of players, particularly that of *goal-shy* strikers forced to *plough a lone furrow* while *cutting a forlorn figure* up front. In the absence of on-pitch microphones – surely only a matter of time for those – we must rely on an array of *histrionics* and frenzied gesturing. Football's code of non-verbal communication can be deciphered as follows (see page 78 for visual clarification).

The 'dive' allegation

A one or two-handed paw-like gesture (repeatedly jabbed forward) to indicate an opponent has *gone to ground too easily*. Performed in the direction of the referee, just after an intimidating loom over the alleged diver and an aggressive suggestion that they may wish to get to their feet.

'Nice idea'

Suitable for use only in the formative opening twenty minutes of a match, or if winning comfortably, the raised-hand-into-thumbs-up gesture reassures a team-mate that his overhit, *raking*, fifty-yard *Hollywood ball* was, despite ending up in the sixth row of the stand, a *nice idea*.

The apologetic palm

If a striker selfishly goes for goal instead of passing to a better-placed (and now apoplectic) team-mate, the standard dispute-resolution procedure is the earnest offering of a single open palm.

The grimace

Other than genuine physical pain, the most common, grimace-inducer is a *squandered* goalscoring opening. Be it a *gilt-edged opportunity* or simply a *real chance* – but not an *absolute sitter* – the miss is often accompanied by this pained expression of self-condemnation, pre-empting the co-commentator's pondering over whether the chance-misser will be *left to rue* the missed chance. No other misdemeanour in football can be *rued*, it should be added. Non-goalscoring errors may cause a player or manager to *live to regret* them, though.

The virtual ball

The most comical, frivolous act of mime we see each week in our Anglophone domestic leagues is the 'virtual ball'. To support his claim that he *got some of the ball*, a tackler will form a

The 'dive' allegation

The imaginary card

The virtual ball

The unheard whistle

'Nice idea'

The grimace

The apologetic palm

Football's code of non-verbal communication

The muted celebration   The unrepentant trudge   Checking for blood

The metronome   The beleaguered manager clap

'Straight round'
(extra time only)   Substitution vs Moving ball

circular shape with both hands (more than once, if he really means it). As a general rule, the bigger the ball-shape he makes, the more convinced he is that he made contact with it in the challenge. Rather belatedly, this spectacle is being replaced by the rather more understandable grabbing of the actual ball, held out in a desperate plea to the referee to change his mind.

The imaginary card

It's not clear why, where possible, the players cannot communicate these appeals verbally. It has even reached the point where the ridiculous, pantomime act of *waving an 'imaginary card'* (which has now achieved an absurd level of taboo) is seemingly more of an offence than actually asking the referee to book a player. One of those things – like well-meaning pitch invaders and twenty-one-man brawls – that can (perhaps mistakenly) be filed under *Things Nobody Wants to See*.

The muted celebration

A modern classic, and a product of football's complicated moral code. The *muted celebration* involves the curious spectacle of a player obviously, and quite earnestly, **not** celebrating after scoring a goal against a former club. The stony-faced expression, the reluctant embrace with team-mates unburdened by their employment history and who ignore the goalscorer's calm-down gesture, or – in cases of maximum guilt – a raised hand of apology to the opposition supporters.

Opinion remains divided on the *muted celebration*. Some declare it as *classy* or a *nice touch*, while others find it embarrassingly self-indulgent. Either way, it's now hard-wired into instinctive footballing behaviour.

The unheard whistle

An established classic, for players who kick the ball away after the whistle has been blown. First, the offender will nonchalantly point to his ear and then to the noise from the stands, confident that the sympathetic referee will take no action. If this appeal fails and a yellow card is forthcoming, more zealous pointing to the ear (or both ears, in extreme cases) may be necessary.

The beleaguered manager clap

Time is running out for a team to save themselves in an important game, and the manager is fresh out of ideas. Having stood forlornly on the edge of his technical area, he remembers he has one more tool in his locker – the encouraging clap, delivered with gusto while leaning forward. Barrel successfully scraped, he crosses his arms once again, resigned to defeat and, quite possibly, *the axe*.

The metronome

Anxious for his team to dictate the tempo, a manager will indicate to one of his midfielders to start passing the ball more quickly, by means of wringing both hands repeatedly to the left and right in a sort of seed-sowing motion.

Substitution vs Moving ball

Both very similar gestures, but can be distinguished by any expert in the field of non-verbal football communication. Both involve the cycling motion of both hands together, but performing this above the head (either by the physio or the injured player) is to indicate to the bench that an immediate substitution is required.

The unrepentant trudge

When players are sent off, they seem unable to leave the pitch
without slightly undressing themselves. This can range from the
mere untucking of the shirt or the unravelling of some tape to
the sort of full upper-body nudity made famous by Kevin Keegan
and Billy Bremner in the *ill-tempered* 1974 Charity Shield.

Checking for blood

After a *clash of heads*, one or both of the victims are likely to be
seen to pat the affected area and check their hand for any signs
of blood. A reasonable enough act of self-preservation except,
for some reason, it's always done about twelve times in quick
succession. It's important to be thorough.

'Straight round' (extra time only)

The referee twirls a single (upwardly pointing) finger in the
air to indicate that the teams must switch ends immediately at
half-time in extra time, only to be ignored in favour of *taking on
fluids* (exhausted footballers never simply 'drink some water')
and having a vigorous massage from a flustered physio.

Injuries

In these cynical times of simulation and timewasting, the
following guide can be used to gauge the true severity of a
player's injury:
- Waggly wrist = painful
- Fist-pounding the turf = very painful
- Arm straight up in the air while lying prostrate = excruciating

i. Painful

ii. Very painful

iii. Excrutiating

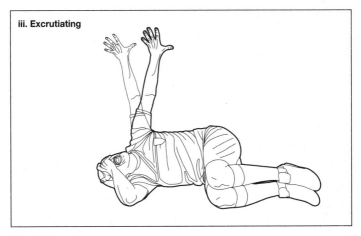

The pain severity guage

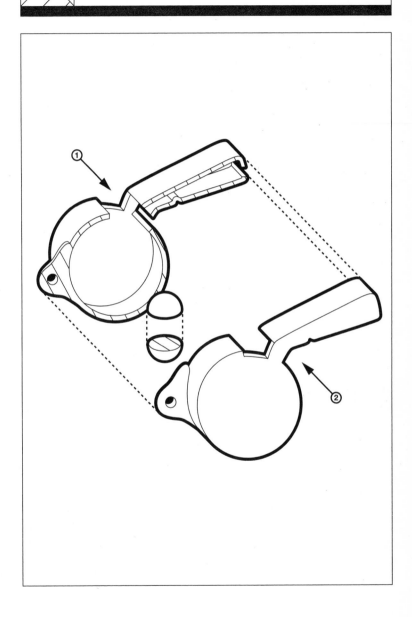

adjudged
/əˈdʒʌdʒd/

verb, past tense
1. considered or declared to be true or the case.

2. deemed to be offside or to have handballed.

6. The Disciplinary Tightrope

Some referees are faultless;[1] some are bastards.[2] While the goalkeeper enjoys his semi-mythical status, the similarly isolated match official enjoys little sympathy as the *man in the middle*. Quite simply: *who'd be a referee*? Always looking a little awkward as they jog around, sometimes backwards, in their spotless astroturf trainers and pulled-up socks, they look very much like dentists and bank clerks. Which, in fact, they traditionally are. They also get very few Christmas cards, apparently.

If they aren't being hated, threatened or – even worse – *harangued*, referees are accustomed to being patronised and ridiculed. Only recently has the era of pressure-cooker professionalism brought an end to broadcasters' quaint practice of mentioning the official's home town before kick-off, which brought the Chester-le-Street*s*, Tring*s* and Orpington*s of this world* their brief moment of fame. Amid the snarling tribalism, there are few more unifying moments than when a referee or one of his assistants falls over, either by stumbling over their own feet while trying to get out of the way or being unceremoniously wiped out while trying to get out of the way. Both scenarios are surely preferable to the referee actually touching the ball during play, an act that grants the aggrieved set of players carte blanche to launch a volley of abuse without the prospect of punishment. Referees should occasionally be seen, rarely heard, but should never, ever make contact with the ball during open play.

With a job widely accepted to be an impossible one, why do referees still struggle to command respect or even the slightest sliver of empathy? Usually, it's because (unlike the millions of Ballon d'Or-polishing hall-of-famers like you and I) *they haven't played the game*. *Consistency*, managers insist, is all that we ask of our officials. This presumably means the application

---

1. Charles Faultless, 1954 World Cup referee. **2.** Segar Bastard, 1878 FA Cup final referee.

of the letter of the law, at which point they are lambasted for not displaying some *common sense* and judging each individual incident on its merits.

To be a referee is to recognise that you simply cannot please all of the people all of the time. Furious radio phone-in callers demand that officials be '*more accountable*' and be obliged to '*come out and explain their decisions*'. Of course, any referee that

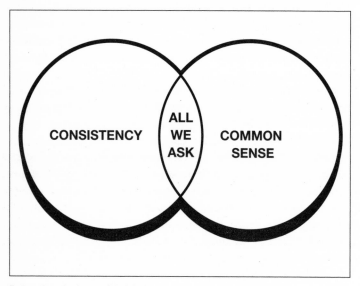

Refereeing: the impossible job

did face the television cameras would immediately be accused of '*seeking the limelight*'. *Card-happy* referees are deemed to have lost control of a game, in contrast to those who *keep their cards in their pocket*; indeed, a premature red card has the potential to ruin a game or, more pompously, *effectively end the game as a spectacle*.

An already knife-edge balancing act is made even more precarious by the studio analysis of their split-second decisions. Irony-proof pundits flirt with self-awareness by recognising the *'luxury'* of being able to pause, zoom, superimpose and virtually recreate, before using all of those privileges to construct a massive 3D truth stick with which to bludgeon the referee to death. Unsatisfied that referees are not infallible and omniscient beings, the coverage of their decision-making further undermines itself with deliberately vague language – offsides are described as *borderline* or *touch-and-go*, it's always just a *suspicion of handball* or a *hint of a push* in the area.

To survive the scrutiny and abuse, officials are forced to close ranks and become increasingly unapproachable. The macho handshakes between a referee and his assistants before kick-off are as much a display of reassuring solidarity as they are a wish for good luck. During the game, the referee's traditional array of emphatic gestures resemble that of an early twentieth-century silent-film actor, but some subtleties must be clarified.

The universally understood gesture for *'nothing doing'* – when a penalty appeal is turned down, despite a *plaintive look* from the supposedly *felled* victim – requires a single forceful uncrossing of the arms with the outstretched hands slicing through the air, not unlike the breaststroke swimming technique. It should not be confused with the *'no more'* gesture, performed at the end of a final verbal warning, which involves a similar arm movement but with the crucial distinction of upward-pointing forefingers. The same digits can be used to identify the two main instigators of a bout of *handbags* and summon them for a brief *ticking-off*.

Persistent offenders find themselves falling foul of *the totting-up process*, which once related to the accumulation of disciplinary points leading to a suspension but now more commonly refers to a number of minor fouls that finally lead to the player being shown a yellow card. In doing so, the referee is obliged to point in the vague directions of where the guilty party's transgressions took place, before sending them on to the *disciplinary tightrope* where it's thereon advisable to be 'careful'.

Cards are *produced* by referees or, in the case of a red one, *brandished*. Sendings-off include such old-fashioned football clichés as a player being *given his marching orders* en route to his *early bath*. The long walk down the tunnel is usually punctuated by the offender kicking out at something, be it an innocent door, wall or water bottle.

At the risk of angering those who insist some referees are still starstruck by the players they officiate each week, there still appears to be room for personality among the elite referees group. Mike Dean's withering looks in the direction of hysterical players can delight or infuriate, depending on your allegiances, while Mark Clattenburg's perpetual expression of mild irritation makes you wonder how enjoyable life as a referee really is. Howard Webb had the approachable authority of a deputy head, a far cry from the schoolmasterly David Elleray who, in the grand old tradition of disclosing referees' day jobs, we all know was actually a Harrow schoolmaster.

On the periphery of proceedings (quite literally, in fact) are the assistant referees, whose previous title of 'linesman' has proven a little difficult to shake off. The 'lino' (this abbreviation tends to work best when angrily querying their decisions) tends to be rather weedier than the main man, although they are armed with a fluorescent flag and *eagle eyes*. Apart from awarding throw-ins, the assistant referee's primary task is to rule on offside decisions. Whether it's *borderline, fractional, marginal,* with or without *daylight*,[3] *half a yard, a yard, a mile* or *a country mile* offside, the assistant referee must get the decision spot on. A wave of the flag can see celebrations *cut short* but runs the risk of disallowing *a perfectly good goal*.

And what about the fourth official (or even the fifth and sixth[4])? It may seem like the easiest job on match day, but

3. The word 'daylight' has never appeared in the official Laws of the Game, but it seems to have been a turn-of-the-millennium by-product of the nebulous concept of *the benefit of the doubt*, which assistant referees are morally obliged to award to attacking players in moments of perceived uncertainty. Indeed, TV replays can even uncover *clear daylight* between a defender and forward, condemning the linesman even further. 4. The poor souls, known as additional assistant referees, are now sent out to the exposed goal-lines without even a flag to wave, leading to passive-aggressive co-commentators openly wondering what it is they actually do, Clive.

these poor, multi-tasking souls must think of some jokes to share with the substitutes before they *enter the fray*, usher fuming managers back into the confines of their technical area, and operate their fiddly digital boards. In the ninetieth minute, the fourth official's climactic moment arrives – he must display the allotted stoppage time. Three minutes? Four? No-one bats an eyelid. But five?! Where did they get five minutes from?!

For many players, the referee exists purely to be argued with, either by way of *haranguing*, *surrounding* (which requires more than one player, otherwise it's just hugging) or *remonstrating*. The futility of arguing with the officials after a decision is laid most bare when a desperate player tries to physically stop a card being produced from a referee's pocket.

Footballers' perpetual sense of injustice means that almost any type of foul is subject to appeal:

The cynical foul

Cynical is used by co-commentators to describe any foul that looks even slightly deliberate. For the perpetrator, there is a hands-up acceptance of his fate, like entering a guilty plea in court. Despite claiming the mitigation of it being his first foul in the match (there's that forefinger again), a yellow card is likely to be forthcoming. If it halts a promising opposition counter-attack, the co-commentator will use his playing experience to confirm that the booked player will quite happily *take that*.

The foul from behind

Perpetually *clamped down* on, in a bid to allow flair players to flourish, but still subject to some of the more frenzied appealing. Meanwhile, the victim curls himself up in the foetal position to ensure his assailant goes into the book.

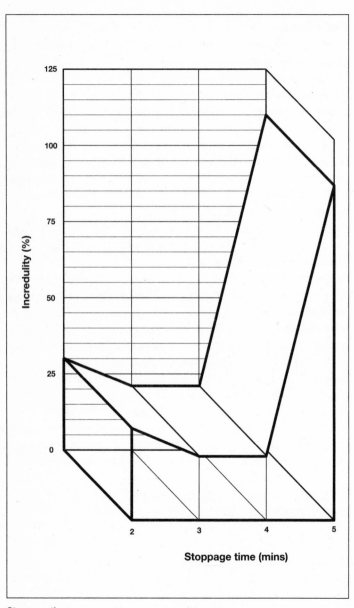

Stoppage time (mins)

Stoppage time

The clumsy foul

Often *clumsy more than anything*, these are always conspicuous by their bumbling lack of *malice*. The guilty party here will attempt to appeal not just after the foul, but during it. The accepted method is to raise both arms above one's head while bundling the opponent over. The wisdom behind this appears to be that if you don't use your hands to bring an opponent to the ground, then it cannot be a foul. An admirable attitude, but one rather at odds with the actual Laws of the Game. Clumsiness within the confines of one's own penalty area is more likely to result in a *stonewall penalty*.[5]

The professional foul

The red card is only halfway to being *brandished*, but the defender knows his fate. Off he goes, possibly by means of an *unrepentant trudge*, during which at least one item of clothing or accessory will be untucked or removed in an instinctive display of displeasure. He has well and truly *taken one for the team*.

Six of one, half a dozen of the other

A *coming-together* or *wrestling match* that lacks a clear instigator may be referred to as *six of one* (this particular cliché is established enough to be left incomplete) or, if the co-commentator is sufficiently leftfield, *six and two threes*. Further TV replays will confirm that the two players were, indeed, *both at it*.

---

5. It is unclear how or why the verb 'stonewall' (to delay or obstruct) became a makeshift adjective for seemingly clear-cut penalties. Perhaps it simply provides a sturdy surface for 'nailed-on' decisions.

Welcome to the Premier League

The standard English top-flight welcome pack for new foreign signings consists of three items: a pair of oversized headphones, a designer washbag and an *agricultural* challenge from an old-fashioned centre-half.

Born out of frustration

Frustration is the mother of many a *rash* challenge, particularly those committed by underserviced and well-shackled strikers. Wayne Rooney is a frequent exponent, suggesting that he himself may have been *born out of frustration*. Similarly, a burning sense of injustice can also inspire rough treatment, and our intrepid co-commentator will confirm that there might have been 'a little bit of retribution there'.

Needless

Few things elicit such irritation from a co-commentator than fouls against players who are going *nowhere*, probably committed by a well-meaning winger who's trying to impress his manager by tracking back.

One of football's crown jewels of perpetually tedious debate, along with managers' handshakes and the *waving* of *imaginary cards*, is diving. Like a sort of footballing Nosferatu, the ever-so-foreign act of *going to ground too easily* is somehow still in the glacial process of *creeping into our game* in order to repeatedly *rear its ugly head*. Serial offenders run the risk of being *branded a diver*[6] or find their penalty-area surges undermined by their pesky *reputation going before them*. Penalty-area *theatrics*, *triple Salchows* (yep, that's how you spell it, apparently) or *going down like you've been shot* continue to be a moral dilemma at football's top level – the beneficiaries quietly consider it a necessary evil, while the victims are reduced to furiously appealing to the referee with an awkward, double-handed squirrel impression.

Football has a range of battlegrounds. Tunnels are the traditional venue for a *fracas*, *bust-ups* are confined to training grounds or dressing rooms, while the touchline is the place to go if you're in search of a good *melee*. It is the sworn duty of a football reporter to faithfully relay the precise number of participants in an on-pitch *brawl*, which is usually *sparked* by an exchange of words.

The rare (but wonderfully alliterative) spectacle of the spit-spat is an excellent case study in football's earnest morality. Should a saliva-fuelled row ever erupt, several self-styled honest pros will insist that they would rather be punched in the face, have their leg broken or have a nuclear warhead detonate in their underpants than be spat at by a fellow professional.

Once the villains of a piece have been dragged to their personal hearings to face an *FA rap*, the language of these disciplinary proceedings is fittingly violent – managers and players can be *slapped with a fine* and *hit with a ban*.

---

6. *Branding* is very much the opposite of *dubbing*. Modern football history is littered with charming, generous and downright outrageous acts of dubbing – at least a dozen diminutive Argentinians have been dubbed 'The New Maradona', while Romanian legend Gheorghe Hagi was dubbed 'The Maradona of the Carpathians'. Other dubious geographical Diegos include 'The Maradona of the Bosphorus' (Emre Belozoglu), 'The Asian Maradona' (Ali Karimi) and 'The Maradona of Basingstoke' (Cristian Levis).

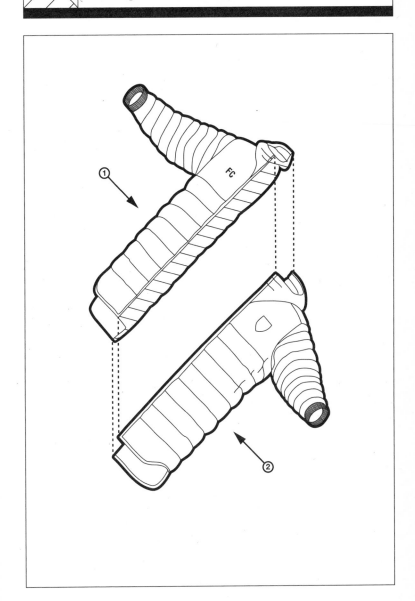

beleaguered
  /bɪˈliːgəd/

  verb, past participle
  1. put in a very difficult situation.

  2. soon to be back on the *managerial merry-go-round.*

7. The Managerial Merry-Go-Round

The modern football manager is the ultimate multitasker. There are forlorn strikers for him to *put an arm around*, there are water bottles to swig from at the precise moment the camera is focused on him and there are virtually-powerless fourth officials to *berate*. All while *kicking every ball*. They once only had to be *philosophical in defeat*, but now they must establish their own *philosophy* for their players to *buy into* in order for *the project* to succeed.

The stresses of management begin in the very first press conference where, with great seriousness, his 'performance' in answering routine questions is presented as some sort of benchmark for his potential success in the job. Christian Gross's infamous Tottenham travelcard in 1997 ('the ticket to my dreams!') remains one of the few high-profile cases of a new manager bombing in his first press-pack engagement.

The technical area – which is *prowled* by its inhabitants – is one of the main stages for the football pantomime. If the manager isn't busy being *animated* or *deep in conversation with his No. 2*, then his thoughts are probably on sale for a penny.

Handshakes between managers at the start of a game, unlike the cursory greetings between the shuffling lines of players, can often become lingering clinches of solidarity, with whispered sincerities that we can never quite make out, ended finally with a brief battle of patronising one-upmanship over who can pat the other on the head last. After the game, of course, such an embrace can be conspicuous by its absence, which can cause a fuss known (rather inevitably) as a *Handshakegate* (see diagram on page 98).

The half-time team-talk usually exists purely in hypothesis. A well-timed goal just before the interval serves not only as football's ultimate *psychological blow* but also to send the beneficiary's team-talk out the window. On the other hand, a struggling

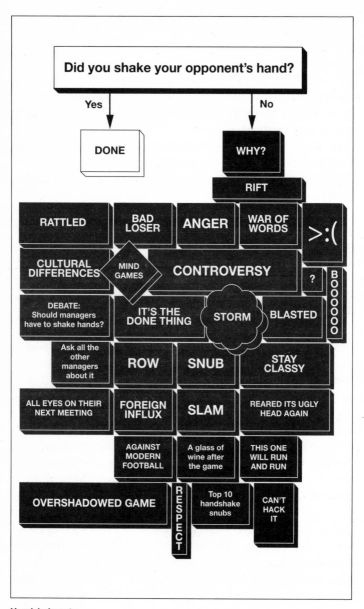

Handshakegate

side may come flying out of the traps in the second half, compelling one of the commentators to reveal, helpfully, that '*I don't know what the manager said to his players at half-time, but...*'

Whatever it was, the words are apparently still ringing in the ears of the scolded players. Much like *handbags* is a curious umbrella term for mild on-pitch disagreements, a lively half-time exchange of views is traditionally characterised by *teacups*, which may or may not have been *flying around* depending on whether he's that sort of manager. Team-talks become much more problematic if the manager suddenly realises that he has *lost the dressing room.*

Approachable and/or amusing new managers (every joke in a press conference is somehow the funniest thing a football journalist has ever heard) are heralded as *a breath of fresh air*, an accolade also given to their team by extension. This is a short-lived honour – the gestation period of familiarity-bred contempt is rather brief in football – but it can be a precursor for being that season's *surprise package.*

Surprise packages, their lungs full of that proverbial fresh air, bloody the nose of a *big gun* early on, and find themselves hitting the early heights in the *embryonic league table*. It is at this point that their all-smiles manager is floated on the football cliché exchange and sees *his stock rise*. With their brand of football having won some friends (and a few points), the surprise package tends to wind down in the final weeks of the season. They may not realise it, but this represents the very early symptoms of what is to become full-blown *Second Season Syndrome*, which manifests itself in a general sense of having been *found out* after losing the *element of surprise* of their first campaign.

In a modern game obsessed with cash, there are other loosely defined currencies that keep the football world going round. *Credit* is awarded either in *full* or, at least, *not taken away from plucky* teams. *Class* (or *classiness*) is governed by football's high horse-riding moralists who hover around post-match interviews keeping an ear out for any bad losers. Finally, there

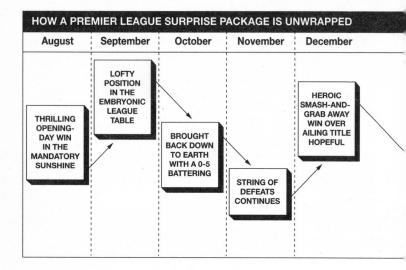

HOW A PREMIER LEAGUE SURPRISE PACKAGE IS UNWRAPPED

August	September	October	November	December
THRILLING OPENING-DAY WIN IN THE MANDATORY SUNSHINE	LOFTY POSITION IN THE EMBRYONIC LEAGUE TABLE	BROUGHT BACK DOWN TO EARTH WITH A 0-5 BATTERING	STRING OF DEFEATS CONTINUES	HEROIC SMASH-AND-GRAB AWAY WIN OVER AILING TITLE HOPEFUL

is *pressure*, a concept which seemingly exists purely to power the *managerial merry-go-round*. Depending on their team's performances, pressure on managers can be *mounting*, *piled on* or *eased*. None of which matters, though, because the *under-pressure* (or *under-fire*) boss – who's *never walked away from anything in his life, and isn't going to start now* – insists that he *thrives on it*.

It's possible to pinpoint the exact moment a manager officially becomes *beleaguered*. The perimeter of the technical area suddenly becomes a precipice as he stands all alone, offering only the occasional earnest hand-clap (see Chapter 5). He's already hailed the fans as '*magnificent*' (which may buy him a few more weeks) and repeatedly *can't fault the effort* of his players but, with no cards left to play, stands on the brink. His team's form book was defenestrated in a briefly heroic cup run that merely *papered over the cracks*. He billed his side's upcoming matches as *cup finals*, and his team didn't win any of them. A gleeful, booming chorus of 'SACKED IN THE MORNING' is heard from among the opposition fans (or, in extreme cases,

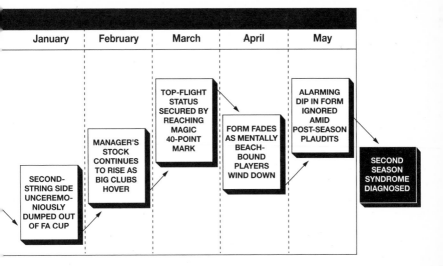

January	February	March	April	May
SECOND-STRING SIDE UNCEREMO-NIOUSLY DUMPED OUT OF FA CUP	MANAGER'S STOCK CONTINUES TO RISE AS BIG CLUBS HOVER	TOP-FLIGHT STATUS SECURED BY REACHING MAGIC 40-POINT MARK	FORM FADES AS MENTALLY BEACH-BOUND PLAYERS WIND DOWN	ALARMING DIP IN FORM IGNORED AMID POST-SEASON PLAUDITS / SECOND SEASON SYNDROME DIAGNOSED

his own), as a brave cameraman acquaints the nation with his nostrils. He slaves all week over his tactics whiteboard only for the shouty TV reporter to ask 'what's the thinking there?' and he's visibly had enough. The *knives are being sharpened, the axe* is being readied and he's about to *get the bullet*. It's either a blessing or a curse for managers that their aptitude for the job is measured in so many vague ways, the most tangible metric of all being the league table – the designated bottom line for the *results business*.

The *sack race* (not actually a race, and not nearly as fun as it sounds) usually begins in around early December. Once one club finally puts their flailing manager out of his misery, others tend to follow fairly quickly. Most of these stories are a predictable cascade of media-driven events, which can be simply condensed (see page 105 for visual representation).

A struggling manager passes through several phases before he finally gets the axe: *pressure* comes first, which then finds itself buried under the misery piled on after a particularly abject performance, ideally against lower-league opponents in a

Second Season Syndrome

domestic cup competition. At this stage, the manager in question is now officially under fire, which often prompts *the dreaded vote of confidence*[1] from the club *supremo*.[2] Now everybody knows he's facing the axe, and his name takes on the prefix of *beleaguered*. Rumours surface, which no one needs to bother substantiating, that the *dead man walking* now has *six games to save his job*. It's pretty much always six games, suggesting that the League Managers Association once flexed their trade union muscles and insisted on a minimum term for this speculative ultimatum. Once this industry-standard stay of execution has been observed, the official club statement is typed up in earnest.

The sheer number of manager sackings has led to a strict script to which official club statements must adhere. Such statements are apparently bound by FA regulations to include the following:

Acting now in the best interests of the club

Once the requisite six games to save his job have passed without a reversal in the manager's fortunes, the club have a race against time to edge him out of the revolving door before the next transfer window flies open.

Thanks for efforts

Always *placed on record* (not, sadly, in the musical sense), a half-hearted appreciation of the efforts of the underperforming manager – however fruitless they were – is extended.

---

1. The *vote of confidence* became so clichéd that it is now the *dreaded vote of confidence*. Unfortunately, that in turn has become a cliché. A wonderful example of the evolution of a football phrase, where any attempts at self-awareness are resisted. **2.** *Supremo* is an endangered species in the jungle of football clichés, which is a shame for such a pointlessly spectacular word.

Well-wishing for the future

Knowing full well that the poor ex-manager (not literally poor, thanks to his bumper pay-off) will have to take a downwards step to resurrect his career, a club can safely wish him well for the future in the knowledge that he probably won't be back soon, in a rival's hotseat, to bite the hand that used to feed him.

Hope to appoint a new manager as soon as possible

A rather redundant sign-off from the newly managerless club, reassuring their fans that hiring a replacement is at the top of their to-do list.

If a replacement hasn't been lined up, a stop-gap option is frequently needed. The caretaker manager, historically an easy, tracksuited target for ridicule, has now been carefully rebranded by football's new era of corporate seriousness as the tough-talking interim manager. The average interim manager finds the *hotseat* to be a stressful rollercoaster ride, even if they manage to secure a win in their first game in charge, after which they are inevitably asked: '*It's easy, this management lark isn't it?!*'

Replacing a manager sounds like a right pain in the backside: scribbling together tinpot statements, drawing up shortlists and identifying targets, having to get permission to talk to employed managers (before being refused that permission in a mardy, short-lived stand-off), interviewing candidates (what on earth are they asked?), before finally making their man sit under a proverbial veil before his debut press conference. Then he has to be handed a *war chest* – and where can you get one of those these days?

Much like the sack race, the *managerial merry-go-round* isn't quite as exciting as its name suggests. It's populated by managers, itching to get back into the game, who crave the matchday buzz. Some, like Gerry Francis, even forget to update

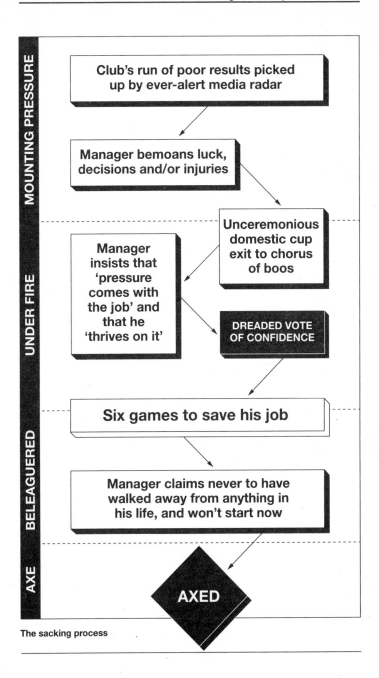

MOUNTING PRESSURE

Club's run of poor results picked up by ever-alert media radar

Manager bemoans luck, decisions and/or injuries

Unceremonious domestic cup exit to chorus of boos

UNDER FIRE

Manager insists that 'pressure comes with the job' and that he 'thrives on it'

DREADED VOTE OF CONFIDENCE

Six games to save his job

BELEAGUERED

Manager claims never to have walked away from anything in his life, and won't start now

AXE

AXED

The sacking process

their hairstyle. Others eventually lose faith and, despite not officially retiring, drift towards media work (the early-morning shift on Sky Sports News is the entry-level position) or vague-sounding 'ambassadorial roles' at one of their former clubs.

The *managerial merry-go-round* operates all year round, both to keep unemployed managers in the loop and to service the revolving doors of the increasingly trigger-happy clubs. It steps up a gear whenever a vacancy is publicised. The speculation begins when someone is *installed* as the bookies' early favourite for the job (the successful applicant is also *installed*, making football managers sound more like kitchen cabinets). However, despite the plentiful supply of willing managers, finding the right candidate can be far from straightforward. Between the axe and the unveiling lies the swamp of speculation.

Speculation is the lubricant, if you will, for the *managerial merry-go-round*. Already-employed managers rule themselves out of the running for whichever *poisoned chalice* is on offer by either *pouring scorn* or *cold water on speculation* and then *calling for an end to* it. Meanwhile, rumours exist merely to be *scotched*, *quashed* or *laughed off*, talk of a potential move is *dismissed* and reports are *rubbished* (a verb almost exclusive to football). More bashful press conferences may witness the manager attempt to *distance himself from speculation* or *remain coy*, but not before admitting that he's 'flattered' by the links.

Those tempted by a vacancy, but bound by some sort of code of honour, insist that they '*can't comment on something that has nothing to do with me*', which is gleefully interpreted as *refusing to rule themselves out*, which in turn succeeds only in *fuelling speculation*.

The standard method for a manager to declare his interest in a vacancy is to *throw his hat into the ring*. The interim manager generally gets the first throw of the hat, despite not having any realistic long-term prospects. Otherwise, one wonders just how many dispensable hats Alan Curbishley has in his collection.

Talk ensues of funds being made available – possibly enough

to fill the aforementioned *war chest* – but supporters should no longer expect him to hit the ground running on his debut. The cruel gods of football fate cottoned on to this trick a while ago, after Premier League chairmen started firing managers every other week in the hope that the replacements would automatically win their first game in charge. If he arrives in the job immediately before a fixture, a new manager may wish to take *a watching brief* in the stands for his first game, during which he will be given ample opportunity to realise the *size, enormity* or *magnitude of the task on his hands*. A 1-1 draw is generally considered acceptable nowadays, particularly for a side who can sit back and relax in its new status as a side *in transition*. Being *in transition* is effectively the pure football equivalent of going into administration – you can kiss goodbye to around ten points straight away, but it gives you a bit of breathing space.

Until, that is, the mutually consensual axe falls once more.

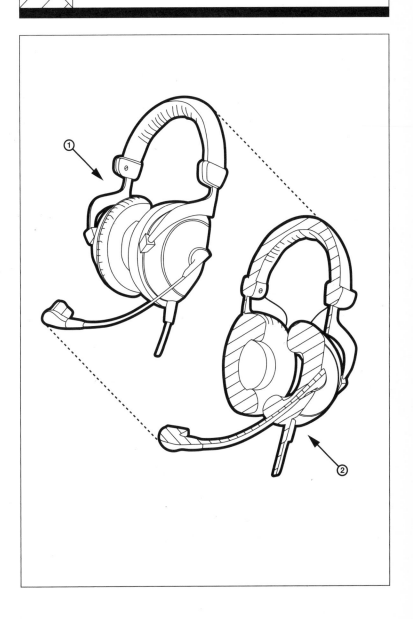

absorbing
/əbˈzɔːbɪŋ/

adjective
1. intensely interesting; engrossing

2. televised, 0-0, half-time.

8. For Me, Clive: The Pundits and Commentators of this World

It may be hard to contemplate the scenario of too much football, but TV football is perilously close to saturation point. A typical Premier League weekend can see around twenty hours of live coverage and highlights and (once you take out the super-slow-motion footage of players disembarking their team bus clutching a washbag and waving sheepishly at an unidentified acquaintance in the tunnel) there is a huge dependence on football-speak to fill this airtime.

The broadcasters take themselves, and their multibillion-pound contribution to football's exponential growth, extremely seriously. If anything before, during and after the game can be caught on camera, it will be – with the surprising, continued exception of the sanctuary that is the dressing room, in which all goings-on can merely be speculated about back in the studio. What's more, the broadcasters are well aware that there isn't *really* four hours' worth of interesting content to dedicate to a football match and know they can get away with a sensational amount of waffle. Faced with an overwhelming ratio of filler to killer, football pundits become easy targets for ridicule, but this is undoubtedly an environment where cliché must be allowed to flourish.

There are occasional laments about football's TV coverage but, with little consensus on what constitutes the best approach to studio analysis, we can only assume that badly lit, wobbly-camera interviews with the *key men* and orchestra-backed montages of previous meetings between the two teams are what viewers actually want.

Over the last decade or so, we have been bombarded with technology to keep us tuned in either side of the game. Jamie Carragher and Gary Neville's weekly games of chess-paced virtual air hockey take place on gargantuan touchscreens, while arrows are superimposed on to freeze-frames of the action until they start resembling the opening titles of *Dad's Army*.

While many pundits are criticised for their lack of insight, those who do try to delve a little deeper are considered boring. The hour-long build-ups on Sky Sports allow them to play around with Premier League minutiae to their hearts' content, while the considerably more compressed format of *Match of the Day*, for example, rarely allows more than a summary account of each game (with a few superficial graphics thrown in for effect). Where ex-players used to retire to go and run country pubs, they are now finding new careers in the football media. There's a place for almost everybody somewhere in the TV football food chain: the early-morning guest opinion slot on Sky Sports News (for your more jaded ex-pros like Tony Gale or the managerial merry-go-round's Alan Curbishley), a seat on the once-great but now irrelevant *Football Focus* (for ambitious player-pundits like Martin Keown or Kevin Kilbane), or even entry to football's inner circle of braying banter, *Soccer Saturday*.

There seems to be an assumed need for these roles, but what are they actually *for*? Why are they all employed to do lots of talking without actually *saying* anything? There is football on somewhere, somehow, whenever you want it, but what remains to say about any given ninety minutes that hasn't been said before?

Studio punditry is traditionally a two-man concern – rising to three, or even four, if the occasion demands it – one of whom will be introduced as 'someone who knows a thing or two about' the specific fixture or competition being covered that day. We've become accustomed to the formal dress code, with ever-enthusiastic Sky pundit Jamie Redknapp's three-piece suits a regular feature, occasionally supported by the 1999 winner of *Britain's Best Dressed Man*, Dwight Yorke. And there they sit, directing a frequent thumb towards the pitch behind them in case we forget what on earth it is they're talking about, the mise en scène completed with half-empty glasses of mineral water and bits of paper strewn across the Perspex table. Polysyllabic foreign names are a source of great mirth among the more old-fashioned pundits – '*easy for you to say, Gary!*' – as are any self-deprecatory remarks about their lack of pace, fitness or goalscoring prowess during their own playing career. Paul Scholes's retirement in 2013, however, robbed punditry of some guaranteed chuckles over his mistimed tackles.

Much of the build-up is focused on the main protagonists of the upcoming match. All-important live footage of the player warming up is accompanied by some meaningless platitudes about his importance to his club. Where 'world class' once sufficed as an indication of a player's accepted quality, a slightly more complex system has emerged for rating footballing ability, seemingly inspired by the disposable razor blade.

Gillette developed the first safety razor in 1903, and a single blade was deemed sufficient for almost seventy years, until the *Trac II* featured a sensational second blade. In 1998, a third blade appeared in the form of the *Mach3*. Fierce competitor Wilkinson Sword took only five further years to squeeze in a fourth cutting surface with their *Quattro* range, before Gillette came roaring back in 2006 with the *Fusion*, which boasted a game-winning fifth blade.

Similarly in a state of perpetual dissatisfaction with their lot, cutting-edge football pundits have followed a similar curve. Perhaps motivated by the Premier League's foreign influx of talent that began in the mid-1990s, West Ham manager Harry Redknapp popularised the use of '*top player*', a phrase that could be modified to adjust to the standard of player in question. The mid-2000s saw the addition of a second '*top*' – pioneered by Harry's son Jamie – as the world's '*top, top players*' started to arrive on our shores. As other pundits begin to adopt and master this new subtle approach to appraising elite football talent, Redknapp Jr recently broke new ground with the concept of a '*top, top, top player*'. With more and more time to fill in

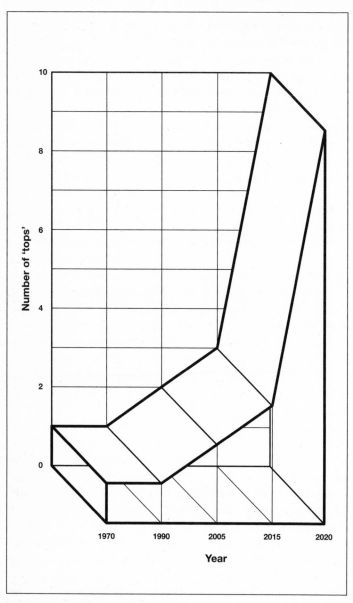

Projected growth of punditry 'top' usage

the schedules, the potential for growth here is surely limitless, as the chart (shown left) illustrates.

One grammatical device that comes in handy when pundits are forced to rack their brains for illustrative examples is the curious plural. Citing *the* Arsenal*s, the* Chelsea*s* and *the* Manchester United*s* (sometimes *of this world*, for extra clarity) somehow manages to subtly pad out the evidence. Made-up or corrupted terms like '*lacksadaisical*'[1] and '*chomping on the bit*'[2] go unchecked, embedding them deeper into the football language. The contents of a player's *locker* are always analysed positively while replays of a well-taken goal are helpfully backed by a gloriously unnecessary statement: '*that's what he's capable of*'. Well, clearly.

Much like any decent football squad must find that perfect blend of youth and experience, so must the broadcasters combine the right amounts of curmudgeonliness, earnestness, and suaveness. Alan Hansen's slurred, growled adjectives were covered in Chapter 4 and, without his guidance, we'd never have known that certain things on a football field are liable to happen '*time and time again*' or what is in fact '*the one thing that defenders hate above all else*'.

Of all the people on the football broadcasting front line, it's perhaps the commentator who gets the easiest ride from the armchair critics. For them, the language of football exists for economy and for clarity, albeit with the occasional tired fallacy. They will still claim, when penalties are looming,[3] that they are *a lottery* and that a team *are at their most vulnerable when they've just scored*, but these observations are not designed to stand up to scrutiny. Similarly, exclaiming that 'Messi is human after all!' and that a stray Xavi pass is some sort of *collector's item* is just grist for the commentary mill.

Some quaint practices – such as giving a brief early-exchanges summary to '*anyone that's joined us late*' or holding

---

1. The excellent *Football Lexicon* (John Leigh and David Woodhouse, 2004) recognises this 'variant form [which] seems to be allowed, perhaps by contamination with *lax*'. **2.** As opposed to the correct *champing at the bit*. See also: *stamping ground* vs *stomping ground*, which admittedly is a rather less clear-cut affair. **3.** Penalties always 'loom', while extra time 'beckons'.

the erratic foreign TV director responsible for European night action-replay indulgences – have faded, replaced by scripted alliteration (Peter Drury's 'HISTON! HISTORY! *HYSTERIA!*' arguably contributed to the diminishing *magic of the FA Cup*) and lame dad jokes. Comfortingly, though, they still greet pitch invaders and twenty-one-man brawls with the out-of-touch observation that '*nobody likes to see that*'. We bloody do. Similarly, no one's falling for the old *intriguing game* act at half-time – it's not been *absorbing*, it's not been *fascinating* – it's been shite.

Many have perfected the art of honing a voice that is both inoffensive and sufficiently unique at the same time – to the point where it became rather unnerving if you ever caught a glimpse on camera of an Alan Parry, a Jon Champion or a Peter Drury, voices you never even considered had faces to accompany them.

And then, over on ITV, there's Clive Tyldesley. Annoyingly, it's very difficult to study him without descending into Clive clichés: yes, he has a certain affinity to Manchester United and a vivid memory of the 1999 Champions League final. Both are understandable and, with a little perspective, even tolerable. But Tyldesley's commentary traits are more subtle than that. Wry understatement is Clive's bag: 'A small matter of a certain young man by the name of David Beckham – whatever happened to him?!' A veteran of a frankly ludicrous twenty-nine major finals, he deserves respect for his sustained spell as ITV's number-one man but, unfortunately, his familiarity has fathered a fair bit of contempt. Clive undoubtedly means well – his pretend conversations between members of the crowd caught on camera (as well as his surreal depictions of the nation's children negotiating revised bedtimes when a cup game goes beyond ninety minutes) are, at worst, the harmless efforts of an embarrassing dad rather than a rampant egotist.

Meanwhile, up in the gantry, co-commentary is in crisis. Andy Gray cackled his way off British television, Trevor Brooking went and got a proper job with the FA, and David Pleat seems to have all but disappeared. Those remaining face a barrage of criticism from all angles whenever they pick up a mic.

What are they actually there for anyway? There's already someone there, with hundreds of games under their belt, to tell you what's happening right now – why the need for someone else, with considerably less formal broadcasting training, to tell you what's just happened? If necessity is the mother of invention, what keeps giving birth to this irrelevance? Anyway, they're here, telling us if an injured player is still moving *gingerly*, which manager will be *the happier at half-time* and that, *in many ways, that away goal hasn't changed* your team's job very much.

At the forefront of this peculiar trade is ITV's Andy Townsend, a perfect example of a co-commentator whose apparent importance to his employers seems to directly correlate with Twitter opprobrium.

Freed from the confines of his ill-conceived Tactics Truck when ITV relinquished top-flight highlights back to the BBC in 2004, Townsend has cemented his place as terrestrial television's most prominent co-commentator. Townsend is very much the anti-Pleat, communicating not in meandering monologues but in staccato bursts of gritty sentiment. 'G'won,' he mutters, an indication that a shooting chance is very much available. 'That's better,' he offers, sometimes up to half a dozen times in ninety minutes, to midfielders slowly managing to locate *the scruff of the* game's *neck*.

None of this is particularly insightful from a man who captained a team at a World Cup, of course, but it adds something to the commentator's observations rather than just repeating them with slightly different words – there's genuine conviction there, even if it's misdirected. Whenever Townsend is in front of the camera, he's continually nodding or poking an earnest thumb at the pitch behind him – he longs to be back out there, but must settle for the next best thing. He lives vicariously through the younger men playing in front of him, urging them to '*get in and around*' their opponents.

Perhaps he is a victim of English football's forced Enlightenment, ushered in after various schoolings in major tournaments from sides capable of keeping metronomic possession, and a time where grit and determination alone just won't cut it. Once again, though – what exactly do we want from our co-commentators?

The French call them 'consultants', in Italy they provide the *commento tecnico*, while in Scandinavia they're known as 'expert commentators'. Ostensibly, co-commentators are employed for their inside knowledge but, more often than not, they appear to be masters in the art of stating the bleeding obvious.

There's not really much chance of you becoming a co-commentator if you don't have a regional accent and haven't had a *journeyman* career in and around the top flight. However, if you do possess the relevant qualifications, you may be inte ested in this minute-by-minute guide to your new career. These instructions will prepare you for any scenario or eventuality that requires your verbal intervention. What to say, how to say it and what not to say – it's all here.

2 min: 'Good evening everybody' (© David Pleat). Once the commentator has eased us into proceedings, you'll be needed to offer some early tactical observations – simply confirming the positions of a couple of attacking players will suffice here.

6 min: The offside flag goes up. Wait for the replay, so you can reliably judge the assistant's call, and then describe it, incredibly unhelpfully, as *borderline* or *touch-and-go*. Don't use the visual tools at your disposal to decide one way or the other – that's not what the viewers are looking for at all.

9 min: Who's *made the brighter start*? If unsure, claim that both teams are *cancelling each other out* or perhaps even *feeling each other out*.

11 min: One of the goalkeepers, who happens to be from mainland Europe, *elects to punch* a couple of crosses away. This is a clear indication that he's hugely *uncomfortable under the high ball* and must be subject to further aerial testing to establish if, indeed, he *doesn't fancy it*.

15 min: The possession stats pop up in the bottom corner of the screen. *Look at that!* you must instruct us, because we're stupid and we don't know how to use our eyes. *That's to be expected*, you assure us, as we breathe a collective sigh of relief.

16 min: Someone tries a speculative effort from thirty-five yards that flies wide. Regardless of who the goalkeeper is, they'll *have to do a lot better to beat a goalkeeper of his quality from that distance*.

18 min: Penalty shout! Armed with a couple of slow-motion replays and a vague understanding of the Laws of the Game, you conclude that there was *minimal contact* with the optional suffix of ... *for me*.

20 min: A second player in quick succession slips – or, rather, *loses their footing* – on the *greasy surface*, which you will use as ammunition to bemoan *these modern boots the players are wearing these days*.

22 min: A free kick is awarded, just left of centre, twenty-five yards from goal. It's going to be one of those new-fangled free kicks that are so in vogue nowadays with the modern, lighter football, and you feel obliged (once again) to explain the technique to us in the sort of way our grandma might try and describe a PlayStation. In summary, though, the ball needs to go up and then down again, which may or may not be achievable from various distances.

23 min: The free kick enters near-earth orbit to a highly audible chant from the opposition fans of 'what the fucking hell was that?' It's too loud to ignore and too profane to mention, so you go a bit quiet for a few seconds instead.

26 min: The game enters a lull, allowing some time for some joshing with the commentator about his age (specifically, the fact that he can remember things that happened a long time ago) or his fashion sense.

30 min: The woodwork is struck! How unlucky is that?! '*Desperately unlucky*', that's how. That cruel, cruel, static, regulation-size goal-frame.

31 min: *He could have had a hat-trick already,* you claim, based on very flimsy logic indeed.

34 min: Another penalty shout! Just *a coming-together*, you decide, as the referee waves away the appeals. *If you give that*, you sagely point out, *you'd be giving 10–15 penalties a game*. Nobody's ever discussed the relative merits of such a scenario, though.

37 min: You're detecting that the home crowd's *anxiety is transmitting itself on to the pitch* on some sort of secret frequency.

38 min: A radiowaves expert one minute, a degree-level anthropologist the next: you don't think much of the body language of the home side's misfiring striker as he ploughs a lone furrow up front.

40 min: It's been *absorbing* and a *chess match* so far, which is punditspeak for 'not very good but I can't explain why'. The favourites for this game, assuming they have at least *turned up*, just *haven't got going yet*.

41 min: Yellow card! It was *clumsy*. No – sorry – it was *clumsy more than anything*.

42 min: Now you have to diagnose a specific lower-leg injury using only a close-up shot as the player gets to his feet (*gingerly*, no doubt) and hobbles off. The general rule here is: *if it's an impact injury he might be able to run it off, but if it's muscular...*

43 min: He's back on the pitch, but does he look *at all happy*? Is he *moving freely*?

44 min: He's *moving much better now.*

45 min: Time for your first-half summary, delivered with a thoughtful sigh. *It's not been a classic so far*, but the most important thing the commentator wants to know from you is: *which manager will be the happier at half-time?*

46 min: What will the manager of the underdogs (and the happier of the two managers) have asked for at half-time? *MORE OF THE SAME.*

47 min: Oh, look – there's a shot of a legendary ex-player, sat up in the posh seats. They *could probably do with him out there now*, couldn't they? He *knows a thing or two about* putting the ball in the back of the net, eh?!

53 min: One of the visitors' midfielders has impressed you today, *he hasn't put a foot wr*... oops, *commentator's curse*! He sends a crossfield pass into the crowd.

57 min: *Gilt-edged chance* for the home side! But the shot takes an impressive trajectory as it arrows over the crossbar. *If anything*, Clive, *he's almost hit that too well*. (This complex phenomenon is covered in more depth back in Chapter 1, you may recall.)

59 min: *A lesson for any youngsters watching,*[4] as a defender stays on his feet and frustrates the attacker with some expert shepherding of the ball out of play.

---

4. The mid-game curriculum for *any youngsters watching* includes textbook downward headers, goalkeepers or defenders staying on their feet for as long as possible and not standing and admiring your own pass.

60 min: Time for your hour-mark monologue, in which you must openly wonder if one or both of the managers *might be thinking of making a change.*

61 min: Yellow card! His team aren't winning, despite general expectations that they would do so comfortably, and so that tackle must therefore have been *born out of frustration*.

64 min: It's stat time again, but this one's an epic two-part drama. There's a tantalising pause between the home side's attempts on goal and the number of them that were actually on target. You admit that you *can't recall the visiting keeper having to make a save*. They haven't *troubled* him enough, for you.

67 min: Right, that's it – *it's going to take a moment of magic, or a mistake* to break the deadlock in this game. Any straightforward goal will be disallowed from here on in.

72 min: Some *fresh legs* finally *enter the fray*. You urge them to run at the opposition centre-half, who *isn't the quickest*.

77 min: Red card! An awful tackle, which *gets worse every time you see it.* On the first replay, it's a studs-up challenge but, by the fourth viewing, it's a stage adaptation of 1982's Schumacher-Battiston injustice.

82 min: Another penalty shout! It's debatable, but you've *seen them given*.

86 min: You're pressed to select your man of the match. We can't see you playing eeny-meeny-miny-moe on your copy of the teamsheet, but we can just about hear the mental cogs whirring. You plump for a youngster, whose performance will do his confidence the world of good.

89 min: One last chance for the desperate home side but, once again, it's *well over the bar. He was leaning back*. They always are, but you *can see what he was trying to do*.

90 min: Your job here is done. You've added very little of note, and any opinions you did put forward were wrapped up in a jumble of non-committal language that suggested you had no confidence in them whatsoever. Despite being an ex-professional player, and therefore comfortably in the top percentile of the nation in terms of football skill, you haven't been able to shed a glimmer of light on why the players did what they did in the last hour-and-a-half. See you again next weekend.

Congratulations, you're now a fully trained peer of *the* Andy Townsend*s*, Mark Lawrenson*s*, Gerry Armstrong*s*, Davie Provan*s* and Alan Smith*s of this world*. You're a combination of amateur comedian, psychoanalyst, orthopaedic consultant and ex-player. Perhaps it's not such a cushy job after all.

Nowhere in football are its clichés more densely concentrated than in the pre- and post-match interviews. The traditional combination of witless, desperate interviewer and barely willing interviewee ensures a curious conversation-by-numbers that relies overwhelmingly (but not always deliberately) on football's stock words and phrases. Such is the reticence of the average footballer that the interviewer frequently finds himself forced to provide the answer before the question has even finished. '*How crucial was that win?*', '*How good is it to be back?*', '*How magnificent were the fans today?*' he will prompt, near-rhetorical questions that require the standard opening of '*Yyyyyyyeahno...*' (followed by its close cousin '*Yyyyyyeahasisay...*') in response.

Goalscorers

A fair and loyal bunch, strikers '*don't care who gets the goals, as long as we get the three points*', but they can't resist adding that '*it's always nice to score*'. Their self-indulgence only stretches to when, at the behest of the brown-nosing interviewer, he contemplates whether his audacious forty-yard lob was '*one of the best goals he's ever scored*' or if he'll be claiming the goal that relied heavily on a *wicked deflection* off a defender's arse. It's only when they claim not to have known about an upcoming goalscoring landmark until '*one of the lads mentioned it before the game*' that they're really pushing it.

Long-serving full-backs, understandably ill-versed in the art of getting on the scoresheet, resort to hilarious bouts of self-deprecation when confronted over their goalscoring exploits. Allusions to *nosebleeds* are commonplace for those players who '*don't get too many*'.

Goalscoring even has its own grammatical style. Any question about a goal tends to be answered in the awkward-sounding present perfect tense – '*Yeah, I've just hit it and thankfully it's gone in*' – as if the player is living out an endlessly looping action replay. This is popular with goalscoring substitutes, so often asked to provide a retrospective commentary on everything that happened before and during their dramatic contribution, including what their instructions were on the touchline:

'*The manager's just asked me to get out there, put myself about a bit, make a nuisance of myself and maybe nick a goal. And that's what I did.*'

Magnanimous captains

There's a wafer-thin line between humility in victory and simply being patronising. Vastly inferior opponents, whatever the scoreline, have always '*made it hard for us*' while even the happiest of *happy hunting grounds* remain '*tough places to go*'.

There are glimpses of self-awareness when it comes to the more tried-and-tested answers ('I know it's a bit of a cliché but...') as the skipper tries to maintain focus and '*take every game as it comes*'. Even in moments of trophy-winning glory, he remembers to rank the occasion a comfortable second behind the birth of his children.

There's room, however, for embellishment and bare-faced revisionism. When inevitably asked after a heroic comeback if they had thought, at 2-0 down, that the game was over, a defiant captain resorts to bare-faced lying and claims, '*Nah, we never stopped believing. We knew that if we got the first goal...*'

Player returning from injury

Delighted to be back in action after a long injury lay-off, the more melodramatic players will recount how '*there were times when I thought about packing it all in*'.

Potential leg-breakers

Faced with accusations of malice after a tackle that leaves an opponent injured, the guilty party (or, more likely, his manager) will attempt to construct a desperate defence of their character, which usually amounts to nothing more than claiming that they're *not that sort of player* and some mumbling about the things they'd never do to 'a fellow professional'.

Managers

Manager interviews perhaps offer a greater degree of deliberateness in their use of clichés. While their young players come across as rabbits in the media spotlight, the older, wiser managers are well-versed in the art of the post-match interview. Media-savvy bosses (or, at least, those who very obviously like to think so) use clichés so readily that it is impossible to conclude that they aren't fully aware of what they are saying. This perceived level of control over the effect of their own words has led to the curious media construction of *mind games*, a post-1992 concept designed to inject artificial excitement into a title race that may be running low on natural suspense. Mind games can broadly be split into two types:

> **Kidology** – It may sound merely like praise for an opponent, but in the context of a title race, this should be interpreted as an attempt to derail them with their own complacency. In extreme cases, kidology can lead to claiming that one's rivals are indeed favourites for the title, a complex psychological ploy to transfer vague, intangible 'pressure' on to them.

> **Taunting** – Rather more straightforward than kidology, since it involves directly criticising your adversaries. Specifically, questioning the track record of rival managers, in the hope of igniting an unsettling war of words, is the aim here.

The referee is more or less protected from criticism nowadays as the managers bite their lip and claim they *'don't want to say too much, because I'll get into trouble'*, but the odd one can't resist and risks the curious-sounding spectacle of being summoned by the FA to 'explain his comments'.

The smuggest post-match interviews are when the manager has reached some sort of personal landmark, be it a certain number of games or years in the profession. Asked if he is '*still enjoying it*?', the veteran boss can be relied upon to make a flippant remark about his blood pressure, his greying hair or his long-suffering wife.

With managers' positions more precarious than ever in the modern game, many of them rely on the post-match interview as a desperate method of staying in employment. Ready-made, vacuum-packed clichés are called upon when the going gets tough. The nearer the manager gets to *the axe*, the more desperate he becomes. And the more desperate he becomes, the more he uses the F-word: Alan Pardew's clubs become 'football clubs', Mark Hughes's matches become 'football matches'. When Sam Allardyce is in trouble, the Premier League becomes 'the Barclays Premier League'.

The post-match interview, be it with a player or a manager, serves to perfectly encapsulate the painting-by-numbers nature of football coverage. Pre- and post-match, football (if we are honest) just isn't as interesting as Sky's hour-long build-up would have us believe. Therefore, television's bloated balloon of hype must be propped up by the scaffolding of the football cliché.

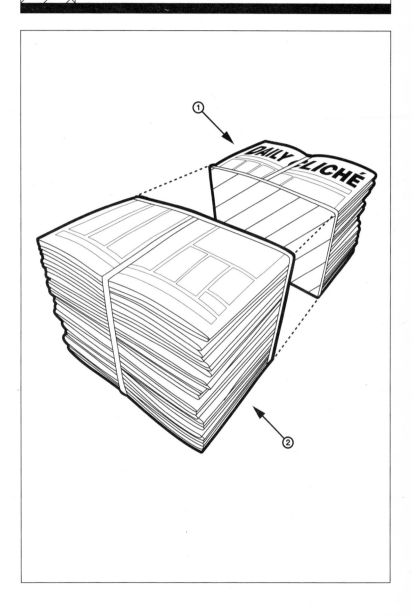

stonewall

ˈstəʊnwɔːl

verb
1. delay or obstruct (a request,
process or person) by refusing to
answer questions or by being evasive.

adjective
1. indisputable, specifically relating to
a penalty kick which the referee had
little or no hesitation in awarding.

9. Aces and Braces:
The Code of Football Reporting

Football has proven unable to survive purely on its own exclusive terminology to describe itself, and has developed a voracious appetite for stealing, commandeering and recycling phrases from elsewhere for its own (invariably clumsy) purposes.

The game possesses a surprising number of obsolete words that originated elsewhere but still flourish here. It doesn't require much sticking out of the neck to suggest that most football fans wouldn't use *stalwart, profligate, adjudged, diminutive* or the verbal form of *rifle* if those words hadn't been given a new lease of life in their adopted sporting context. Nor would they ever describe something being done with *aplomb*, while only the engineers among us could identify a real-life *slide rule*.

While breathless broadcasting is responsible for the more questionable and ham-fisted football clichés, the printed word is where the more refined part of the football vernacular has slowly been allowed to mature over generations. Millions of match reports have had to find a variety of ways to describe goals, horror tackles and emphatic victories.

However, just as a co-commentator must hurriedly cobble together a coherent sentence, newspaper editors have to work within strict limits on their back pages. Economy of space has promoted the use of certain words that are ubiquitous in tabloid headlines in particular, but which you could never say out loud with a straight face (unless you're a Sky Sports News presenter).

Footballers love to be in the headlines, unless *it's for all the wrong reasons*. In an era when pretty much anything players do, on or off the pitch, is liable to be shoehorned into a red-top or internet headline, the football media has developed a set of space-saving keywords (mostly of no more than three to five letters) that account for any incident:

Ace

Where better to start than with the *ace*? Despite its elite con-notations, aceness is a conveniently fluid concept in the world of newspaper headlines. Premier League youth-teamers con-victed of driving offences or League Two players caught in compromising situations in hotels qualify as aces on the basis of sensationalism alone, to the point where using the word to describe those genuinely at the pinnacle of the game seems woefully insufficient.

Axe

The most excruciating wait to be put out of one's misery is when a beleaguered manager (or *boss*, for these purposes) faces the *axe*. In the interests of pedantry, it should be emphasised that managers are never ultimately hit by the axe, they are simply *axed*. It can also be used to describe players being dropped from the squad – not only are they axed, but they are also *frozen out*. It's a cruel world.

Bid

Normally associated with proposed transfer deals, *bid* can also appear as a synonym for a team's efforts to achieve a season-long goal (such as the league title), but without quite the focused determination of a *vow*.

Blast

A vitriolic burst of criticism, with various possible sources or targets – often a poor, defenceless referee.

Blow

A disappointing event, invariably associated with injuries. The *hammer blow*, however, is exclusive to *title bids*.

Boost

The polar opposite of a *blow*.

Coy

'*Tight-lipped*' managers remain *coy* when asked about new signings – talking about players at other clubs (like talking about referees) is something managers go out of their way to say they don't do while still actually doing it anyway.

Dent

A type of *blow*, but one that only affects a *bid* or someone's *hopes* and rarely terminal (unlike, say, a *hammer blow* or a *derailing*).

Eye

Eyeing is the more voyeuristic equivalent of *keeping tabs on* a player, before *mulling over* a bid.

Exit

The departure from a cup competition. If the circumstances are calamitous enough, clubs can also *crash out* of a cup, or even be *unceremoniously dumped out*. Any of which may usher their manager towards the *exit door*.

Faces

After a controversial incident, but before its punishment is meted out, the accused player or club (or soon-to-be-*axed* manager) will be held in the purgatory of simply *facing* their fate.

Hails

Victorious managers feel compelled to *hail* a collective or individual performance, or the vocal support of the (no doubt *magnificent*) fans.

Held

Form-book defying stalemates usually involve a frustrated side being *held*. Sufficiently vague for use with any type of draw, regardless of who scored first or if it was a 0-0 *stalemate*.

Hit

After *facing* an *FA probe* and taking the subsequent *rap*, the miscreant can then be *hit with* a fine (or, indeed, *slapped with* a ban). Also used as shorthand for impressive goalscoring feats ('Ronaldo *hits* four in Real *rout*') or specifically sized capitulations ('Droylsden *hit* for six').

Jibe

The traditionally sneaky opening move in a bout of mind games, which can escalate to a war of words.

Joy

Exploiting its diminutive stature to the full, *joy* is the weapon of choice to describe a manager's/player's happiness.

Probe

The expected preliminary investigations of the FA (or, in more extreme cases, the police) which are invariably *faced* before they are *launched*.

Raid

The act of managers returning to recent former employers to cherry-pick their favourite players, ideally in one single deal. Suggests a certain cynicism from the bidding club, and a level of helplessness on the part of the seller.

Rap

A cult favourite, this diminutive word is far catchier than 'disciplinary proceedings'. An *FA probe* inevitably leads to an *FA rap*, two headline-friendly terms that cannot help but conjure up images rather different to their intended meaning. Such disciplinary proceedings attempt to bring closure to an ongoing *row* of some sort, be it a mere *war of words* or a full-blown, I'd-rather-be-punched-in-the-face *spit-spat*. Even the most serious issues such as *race rows* are effectively trivialised for the purposes of alliteration.

Seal

The rubber-stamping of a transfer deal (*protracted* or otherwise) or the relatively untroubled progression of a club to the next round of a cup competition.

Set for

Similar to facing something, but without the ominous threat, clubs tend to be *set for* cup draws, while players patiently find themselves *set for* a move elsewhere.

Sorry

The equivalent of *beleaguered* for clubs who have capitulated and been very heavily defeated.

Stun

Late or unexpected winning goals have the tendency to *stun*, particularly if Goliath ever faces a tricky trip to face David in the FA Cup.

Switch

A swiftly completed move, unfettered by any prolonged haggling or red tape.

Swoop

Similar to a *raid*, if rather less exciting and more smoothly completed, it again refers to a bigger club signing a player from a smaller club. These can often be bulk purchases, neatly described as *double* or *triple swoops*.

Vow

Nobody in football promises to do anything, they always *vow* – *silencing the boo-boys* is a common vow, as is a player's *repaying* of a *manager's faith*.

Emphatic scorelines also lend themselves to catchy headlines involving vaguely familiar phrases of unclear origin. The fun begins at around the four-goal mark, with a handy hotel-rating analogy:

4 goals = **FOUR-STAR**

5 goals = **FIVE-STAR**

6 goals = **JOY OF SIX/HIT FOR SIX/SIX OF THE BEST**

7 goals = **SEVENTH HEAVEN/SEVEN-UP**

8 goals = (no cliché allocated, although **GR-8** is making a spirited, if clumsy, attempt to establish itself in recent seasons)

9 goals = **CLOUD NINE**

Naturally, we all want to know who the protagonists are in the latest football pantomime, so desperate red-top headline writers can be seen to resort to painful, puzzling abbreviations such as **MOU**, **WENG** or the punned-to-within-an-inch-of-its-life **ROO**.

You won't have to look too hard in tomorrow's papers to find these three- and four-letter codewords and, once you've started spotting them, the more ridiculous they will start to look. Unless the FA's disciplinary panel really *are* spitting sick rhymes from an orbiting space module.

Elsewhere, football's surprisingly subtle relationship with grammar bears curious fruit. While the animal world enjoys an innumerable complement of collective nouns, ranging from the wonderfully alliterative to the impenetrably obscure, you may not be surprised to learn that football has quite a few of its own. For reasons of sensationalism, laziness, inaccuracy or simply diversity, football coverage has demanded that a selection of collective nouns be made available, to be drawn from whenever appropriate. The list covers all aspects of the game and leaves us in no doubt (despite the lack of cold, hard numbers) of how one should pluralise the subjects in question:

Raft of substitutions

The sole domain of largely meaningless international friendlies, where the second half becomes fragmented by the experimentation of both coaches as they seek to give debuts to their *one-cap wonders*. Such games have a tendency to *peter out* until someone finally, inevitably, asks: '*What have we learned?*'

Host of opportunities

Hosts tend to be fairly undesirable collections of missed *opportunities* or *absentees* from the first team.

String of chances

Chances may arrive in *strings*, as can a goalkeeper's saves or a player's impressive performances. Deviating slightly from the grammatical theme, teams will also aim to *string some wins together* or, at the very least, two or three passes.

Brace

A pair of goals for a player in one game, although simply the word *brace* alone is now sufficient, as nothing else football-related arrives in that form. *Braces* can be *quickfire* in nature, but leave the goalscorer vulnerable to be substituted before he can complete his hat-trick.

Flurry of yellow cards

Card-happy referees can sometimes end a barren first half-hour or so by unleashing a *flurry of yellow card*s in quick succession. They will seek to justify this sudden outburst of disciplinarianism by pointing out various areas of the pitch to bemused perpetrators of *persistent fouling*.

Hatful of chances

A more flamboyant exaggeration, used to ridicule the striker that has missed these chances, some of which may have been *gilt-edged*. This represents one of the more imprecise units of measurement in football, as there seems to be no official confirmation of the volume of an average hat. Confusingly, though, while the *misfiring hitman* can fill a hat with *squandered* opportunities, he can also successfully *score a hatful*. Or, indeed, *fill his boot*s.

Run of victories

Similar to a string of wins, but tends to be more smoothly and less desperately put together and, therefore, more suited to a *march towards the title* rather than a *Great Escape* from relegation.

Array of talent

Most commonly found at major tournaments or on *expensively assembled* substitute benches, but can also arrive on a club's youthful *conveyor belt*. The elite clubs, however, often boast a *galaxy of stars*.

Mass of bodies

Generally located somewhere in the midst of an *almighty penalty-area scramble*, a *mass of bodies* can be the reason for a *statuesque* goalkeeper being *unsighted* as a strike from *all of thirty* yards flies through a *forest of legs* and into the net. Elsewhere on the pitch, high-pressing teams coordinate their considerable efforts to form a *swarm of* [insert colour here] *shirts* to win back precious possession.

Embarrassment of riches

To further emphasise the options a manager has at his disposal, the international caps and transfer fees of his substitutes are gleefully totted up to illustrate his *embarrassment of riches*, often (rather aptly) while they are being humbled by a side who were assembled for the price of a four-bedroom house.

Glut of goals

A *goal glut* can occur in a specific competition, particularly a weekend of league fixtures in a single division. We will be excitedly told how many goals *flew in* during the ten or so matches, leaving us to do the maths ourselves to decide if that is actually impressive or not.

Catalogue of errors

The helpful football media dutifully compile these to shame *hapless* individual players at a later date. Alternatively, unfortunate players may wish to browse their *catalogue of injuries* after they've been forced to hang up their boots. It's not just disappointments that are figuratively documented, though – scorers of great goals invariably have a *scrapbook* to keep them in.

Series of high-profile gaffes

A more focused and specific offshoot of the *catalogue of errors*, a *series of high-profile gaffes* tends to be more easily attributed to goalkeepers. The series of *high-profile gaffes* becomes so because Sky Sports News insist on endlessly looping footage of its contents.

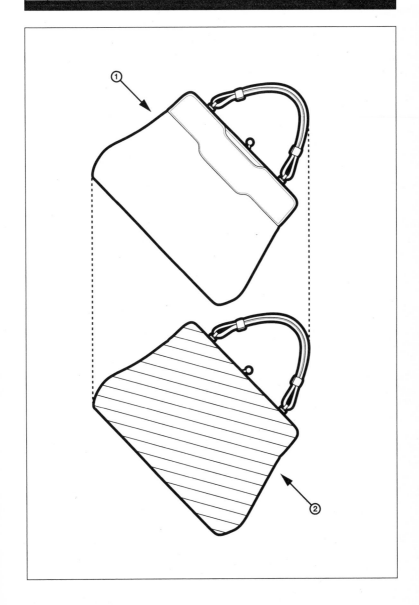

handbags
/han(d)bagz/

plural noun

1. small bags used most commonly by women to carry everyday personal items.

2. a mostly verbal confrontation between two or more players on a football pitch, the physical side of which is limited to foreheads being pressed together and/or some pushing.

10. The Anger Game

Football is boring. The actual football, that is. What keeps the billion-pound TV deals rolling in, though, is controversy. Outrage. *Unedifying scenes*. All the things that *no one likes to see* (but secretly really do) and that 'you', sitting in 'the pub', talk about with 'your mates' after 'the big game'. But football is no longer a game of opinions – it's a game of pummelling other people's opinions into submission in the godforsaken pits of hell that are the comments sections of football websites.

Football is faster, less patient, more highly strung and has more at stake than at any other time in its century-and-a-half history. It's also, therefore, an angry beast.

Outside of its ninety-minute windows, football coverage gorges on a rich diet of injury news, transfer gossip and perpetual controversy.

A variety of *reignited feuds*, *rumbling rows* and *fresh storms* can, if given the right coverage, provide weeks of subject matter, which is particularly useful outside of the frenzied rumour mills of the transfer windows.

The pressures of top-flight football, combined with the sensationalist media that cover it, mean that managers' *tempers can boil over at any point* – and the increasing frequency of outbursts has led to a rich vernacular in football circles. Be it anger directed towards an official, the establishment, an opponent or even their own club, managers' vitriolic flurries are reported in the same predictable way as anything else.

Naturally then, there is a set of words and phrases to account for the full spectrum of footballing anger. The varying degrees of such displays of discontent are displayed in the Anger Severity Scale (ASS) overleaf.

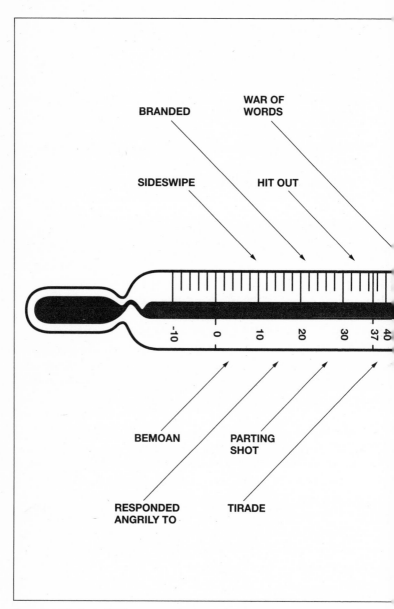

Anger Severity Scale (ASS)

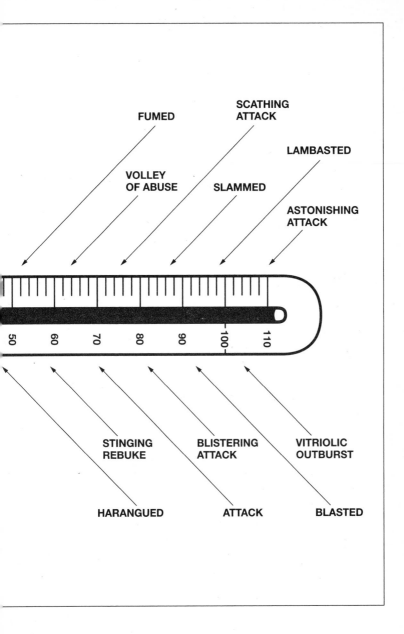

Bemoan

A fairly victimless rant. Managers, particularly those scrapping at the bottom of the table, tend to *bemoan their* team's *bad luck in front of goal*, with injuries, or with 50/50 decisions – although referees are spared direct criticism here.

Sideswipe

A brief, often sarcastic, comment made in a press conference, at the expense of another team or individual. This is lapped up by the gathered hacks, who rub their hands with glee at another ready-made headline. The effect of a *sideswipe* is usually minimal and short-lived, although it can, on occasion, be the catalyst for a *war of word*s.

Responded angrily to...

As managers like to point out, *speculation is part and parcel of the game*. Sometimes though, the rumour-mongers succeed in riling a manager to the point where they feel compelled to *respond angrily to* reports over their future. This is an overreaction; they are far better advised to *laugh off*, *dismiss* or *quash* speculation instead.

Branded

It is at this point that things become slightly more venomous. The soapbox of the post-match interview is frequently used to bring the reputation of an opponent into question. *Branding* is specifically inflicted upon gravitationally challenged opposing forwards, who run the significant risk of being *branded a 'diver'* or even a *'cheat'*.

Parting shot

Departing managers or players, especially in *acrimonious* circumstances, are likely to fire a rather bitchy *parting shot*. Sounding rather like a childish 'didn't like your stupid club anyway' when relations have turned sour, it also functions as a way of ingratiating themselves with their new employers and their fans.

Hit out

An angrier cousin of the act of *bemoaning*, *hitting out* tends to be directed towards a general topic – such as the *influx of foreign players to the Premier League*, for example. More specific targets can include FIFA's clown-in-chief Sepp Blatter, PFA chairman Gordon Taylor or UEFA's Michel Platini.

Tirade

What the *tirade* lacks in explosiveness, it more than makes up for in length and despair. A manager, who feels he has been at the wrong end of one too many controversial refereeing decisions, may *embark on/launch a furious tirade* on the general standard of officiating. A *tirade* is always limited to such general topics.

War of words

A *war of words* can have several causes. It could be instigated by a *sideswipe*, a *parting shot* or being *branded* as something. The newspapers adore a good *war of words*, as it can stretch a very minor story over an entire week. Other elements of a *war of words* are expanded upon below.

Haranguing

Very possibly now included in the Laws of the Game as a specific offence, *haranguing the referee* is an issue that can *rear its ugly head* at any time. Pioneered by the Manchester United's players' vein-bulging pursuit of Andy D'Urso at Old Trafford in 2000 after he'd awarded a penalty against them for Middlesbrough, it has since been adopted by teams up and down the land. There is no official confirmation as to how many players are required for *haranguing* to occur, but I would suggest that a minimum of three protesting players would suffice.

Fumed

Similar to a tirade, although shorter-lived and more likely to be inspired by a specific refereeing decision (the denial of a *stonewall penalty*, for example). The vapour produced by an act of *fuming* may be the *red mist* that subsequently *descends*.

Stinging rebuke

Another important component of the *war of words*. The *stinging rebuke* often has highly moralistic overtones, but is mainly designed to *reopen* a *war of words* or to *reignite* a *feud*.

Volley of abuse

Accompanying shower of spittle optional, the *volley of abuse* has been mastered by the likes of Wayne Rooney. Littered with four-letter words, the volley of abuse is probably the most explicit on-pitch display of discontent.

Attack

Invariably *launched*, *attacks* are as versatile as they are effective. A bog-standard, basic-model *attack* occurs when a manager is far too angry to *bemoan* anything, and wants to make his point quicker than a standard *tirade* will allow.

Attacks can also be *thinly veiled*. These are stealthier than standard *attacks*, and require a bit more spin from the newspapers in order to initiate a *war of words*.

Scathing/blistering attack

The first two rather more volatile forms of *attack* are the *scathing* and *blistering attacks*. A *scathing attack* is more useful for angry disapproval of the behaviour of an individual or organisation. A player may face a *scathing attack* from an opposing manager if he is *branded* a '*diver*', while the FA may well suffer the same fate because of their shambolic disciplinary procedures.

A blistering attack marks the point where a distinct loss of control from the angry party can be identified. Its recklessness, coupled with the notable disregard for the implications of the *attack*, makes it a suitable bedfellow for the *parting shot. Blistering attacks* are a popular weapon of choice for bitter departing players, who may wish to blame their poor form on their former manager and his training methods.

Slam

The most severe form of condemnation an individual can receive. Short, sharp and to the point, a *slam* leaves the media in no uncertainty. As with many other displays of football anger, the *slam*'s effect benefits from the violent connotation of the word.

Blast

A commonly occurring form of footballing discontent, *blasts* can occur on a weekly basis. Similar to the *slam* in many ways, but with a significantly less amount of restraint.

Lambast

Nobody ever *lambasts* anyone outside of football. In fact, given that it also only ever crops up in print, no-one is even really sure how to pronounce it (is it '*lamBAST*' or '*lamBARST*'?)

Nonetheless, if a *lambasting* takes place, then it is surely in response to a heinous misdemeanour.

Vitriolic outburst

Effectively the equivalent of a *volley of abuse*, but within deliberate earshot of the media. Axed managers or frozen-out players are most likely to produce a *vitriolic outburst*.

Astonishing attack

The pinnacle of football anger. While football media coverage is awash with hyperbole, there are a select few adjectives that are still used suitably sparingly – *horrific* injuries are almost always so, for example. *Astonishing attacks* befit their name – they can be directed at unexpected targets at any time. The standard example would be a manager or chairman *launching an astonishing attack* on his own club's protesting fans, who otherwise would be considered untouchable.

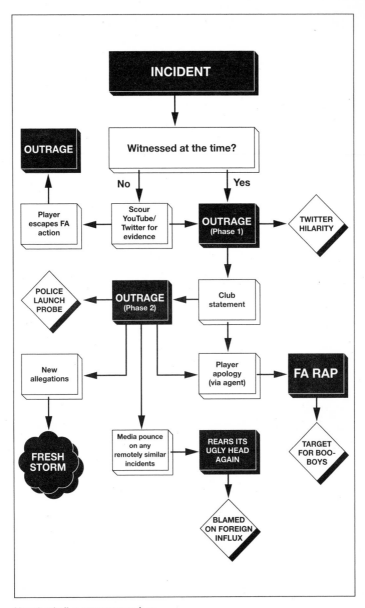

How football controversy evolves

Rather like a transfer saga, but with a much less clear-cut conclusion, a good footballing controversy should *run and run* for as long (and as slowly) as the collective attention span allows. Football offers up a carousel of stock talking points, each referred to as *rearing its ugly head* whenever it should claim a few headlines. The *ugly heads* of modern football include (but are not limited to):

Imaginary card-waving

Almost too preposterous a concept to say out loud, let alone get angry about, the waving of imaginary cards is frequently identified as an unwelcome by-product of *the foreign influx* to these shores. Before 1992, we made do with simply asking the referee to book an opponent – which is fine, apparently.

Diving

Specifically, diving to the extent where a player's *reputation goes before him*, which can only happen once he has been *branded a diver*.

Two-footed tackling

One of those things (like *raising your hands*) that represent *asking for trouble* in football. The debate is unhelpfully spiced up by the mention of *studs showing*, when it's evidently thirteen stone of prime, airborne central-midfielder that does the damage. Such dangerous lunges are billed as *potential leg-breakers*.

These cyclical debates exist to keep Sky Sports News presenters in gainful employment, while just about managing to keep *Football Focus* on the air as it dissects the big issues (with the bluntest of knives) almost a week after everybody else has chewed them over and spat them out.

The evolution of a football controversy is a complicated web of allegations, outrage, statements, apologies and fresh allegations. The original incident – be it a stamp, a gesture or a tweet – is now pounced upon instantly by social media, before even Sky Sports News can mobilise their yellow ticker. Once Twitter has had its first round of fun with the unfolding controversy, the protagonists then find themselves officially *embroiled* in *a row* (although Twitter-based sagas are specifically termed a *storm*). This necessitates the hasty release of an earnestly worded (and Unnecessarily Capitalised) Club Statement that assures the football world that The Football Club are investigating the matter. Should it be a legal matter, the police and the Football Association may *launch* simultaneous *probes*. With the individual at the centre of the row now on the ropes, another blow arrives in the form of *fresh allegation*s, while other (less notable, but broadly similar) incidents are brought to light as this issue officially starts *rearing its ugly head*. In the midst of all of this, keeping things moving along is a secret network of *club insiders*, *close pals*, *senior officials* and *sources close to the player*, who himself may admit things *privately*.

The genesis of a media-based row has had to move with the digital times. Where once players would find themselves constantly and unhelpfully misquoted in *L'Equipe*, they then started taking to Twitter (you always 'take to Twitter' in these circumstances), which has proved itself to be virtual fly paper for outbursts that rate anywhere on the *Anger Severity Scale* (see pages 148–9). The innate immediacy of the platform means that the cooking time for an average controversy is barely longer than the period between the classified scores and the first bars of the *Match of the Day* theme tune. Despite its promise to bring increasingly extraplanetary elite footballers closer to their fans (and with some success), Twitter also represents a constant pitfall for players whose fingers type quicker than their brain works. Ashley Cole's *#BUNCHOFTWATS*, Chelsea team-mate Ryan Bertrand's *#yourfuckingnuts* (both 'later deleted', as is the custom for a good *Twitter storm*) and Sunderland striker Steven Fletcher's pioneering *#headsgone* all gave insights into the psyche

Ashley Cole tweets

of the troubled modern footballer that were more candid and insightful than a thousand pre-match interviews.

Some of the angriest individuals in football are the proverbial *boo-boys*. Booing is a centuries-old method of voicing one's displeasure (but not *derision*, which is delivered in the form of *howls*) and has somehow remained a stalwart of the modern fan's weaponry of outrage. There's no doubt that booing sounds rather effective when tens of thousands of people are doing it but, if you really think about it, the idea of a grown-up shouting 'boooooooooooooo!' is just very, very odd.

There is a flipside to all this vitriol, however. Amidst all the bitterness and tribalism, footballs fans are also quite easily charmed. Any brief glimpse of sportsmanship or compassion is met with the earnest congratulation of '*nice touch*' or, for extra-special moments, '*classy touch*'. Everyone still applauds the ball being kicked back after an injury (although I strongly suspect this is now just a reflex) because, secretly, football loves being nice. It loves it so much that, when faced with unifying incidents such as commemorating the recently deceased, we're queuing up to pat each other on the back for being so thoroughly decent.

However, with more and more money at stake, and more cameras following every *meteoric rise* and *fall from grace*, football seems angrier than ever. From pantomime media stand-offs to vein-bulging abuse of referees, anger has become an integral part of the footballing landscape. Don't expect a collective chill-pill to be swallowed any time soon.

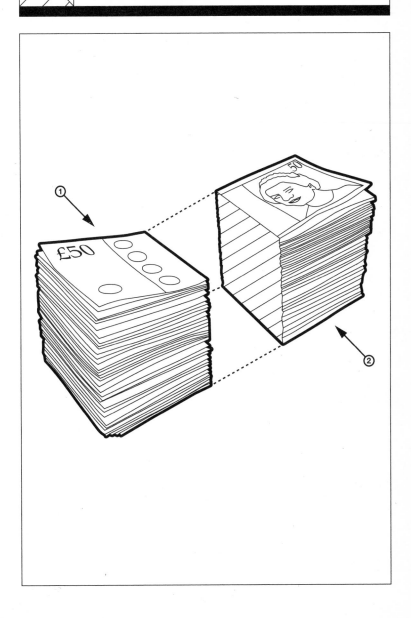

derisory
/dɪˈrʌɪz(ə)ri/

adjective
1. ridiculously small or inadequate.

2. an insufficient transfer bid for a player, as decreed by the owner of the selling club.

11. Beyond Cliché and into the Transfer Window

No one is ever satisfied with their lot. *Transitional phases, rebuilding, clearouts, firesales* – there is always a perceived excuse to dip into the transfer market. It is an endless act of coveting thy neighbour, undeterred by the limitations of the transfer window, and reaching its all-consuming crescendo on deadline day, the secular Christmas Day of football's post-cliché *transfer silly season*.

Like tactics and statistics (but without quite the same intellectualised approach) transfer gossip has developed to become one of football's clearly defined subcultures. It is pervaded by an overwhelming need to know what's happening in the transfer market (ideally before anyone else) and for elite players to switch clubs with enough regularity to avoid everything going a bit stale. The dying breed of the *one-club man* is rarely any use here.

Footballers, like any celebrities, have been commodified to the extent that we feel entitled to know, at all times, what they're up to. And if their lives simply aren't eventful enough we must, by extension, speculate about what they *might* be up to. This is the basis for all transfer rumour.

As a relatively modern concept, transfer gossip hasn't crept its way into the football consciousness over the decades. Yes, some of us remember the flashing, multicolour Clubcall adverts on Teletext (WORLD CUP ACE SET TO SIGN?!) but the rumour mill used to be powered more by vain hope than entitled expectation. Since the adoption of the biennial transfer windows, the phenomenon has grown into a massive beast, which has eaten itself and then proceeded to regurgitate itself back up again – all live on Sky Sports News.

As self-aware as coverage of the transfer window has become, the language involved is more robotic than ever. *War chest*-wielding managers sternly insist that they won't discuss players under contract at another club – an apparently heinous crime which people get oddly tetchy about – before giving in to the media interrogation and finally admitting that the player in question is, after all, very interesting to them indeed. Managers lower down the financial food chain speak of bringing in *new faces* or (in more desperate times) *extra bodies*. *Fresh legs*, however, remain an exclusively mid-game requirement.

The transfer window requires a club to strike with military precision. When a *target* on their *radar* suddenly becomes a *contract rebel*, clubs are said to be on *red alert*. Managers of less glamorous sides must make do with mere *reinforcements*, however, unless they happen to secure a prestigious transfer *coup*.

The flurry of transfer activity in the last days of August leads to a variety of ways that players can be unveiled. The charming image of a player sat at a desk, pen in hand and grinning chairman's arm on his shoulder, appears to be on its way out, in favour of the held-aloft replica shirt.

On deadline day itself, there simply aren't enough in-good-faith rumours to fill the relentless coverage of live transfer blogs, who must resort to hilarious parody reports of players turning up at unlikely sounding airports or, for the purists, motorway service stations. Several degrees of separation, including at least one uncle and a dog, are recommended for adding extra kudos to a spoof sighting of a transfer target.

The last hours of a transfer window are where everything starts to become most self-referential. Crowds gather outside training grounds, no longer in search of a transfer scoop but simply because they are now a mandatory part of the set decoration, behind a flustered roving TV reporter who must take their post-bedtime antics in the best humour he can muster.

Finally, the giant Sky countdown clock enters the *eleventh hour*. Fax machines are biannually dragged back from the brink of technological obsolescence to play a crucial role, things get tangled in the red tape of international *clearance* (which everyone has heard about but cannot explain) before the transfer window *slams shut*, only to gather dust until it *flies open* again a few months later.

Mere rumour is not enough to keep the transfer windows abuzz. Each summer has as its weary centrepiece the arduous narrative of a *protracted transfer saga*. Despite some weary protestations, the media absolutely adore these drawn-out affairs. The newspapers chart the player's on-off move, Twitter provides by-the-minute updates and the increasingly desperate news channels bring it on home. The average protracted transfer saga unfolds thus:

Stage 1 – Keeping tabs

A player reportedly begins to attract interest from several clubs and it emerges that there's no *shortage of suitors*. Scouts are dispatched to *keep tabs* on him, while their clubs continue to *mull over* a possible bid. There's nothing concrete at this stage, so the rumour mill must hedge its bets and link the player with a handful of top clubs, all of whom will be *monitoring* him.

Stage 2 – Red alert

A crucial early juncture. A breakdown in contract talks, or perhaps some stray words from an agent, places the interested clubs on *red alert*. The saga is on.

Stage 3 – The 'hands-off' warning

Never be fooled by its dismissive nature – the *'hands-off' warning* signals a gear-change for the p*rotracted transfer saga* which, in hindsight, proves to be the beginning of the (albeit distant) end. A stalwart of the football vernacular, the *'hands-off' warning* is invariably issued by the player's defiant manager. Unequivocal in his defiance, the naive boss tells the media:

> *'We've had no bids for [Player X] and, to be honest, we wouldn't welcome any. We're not in a position where we need to sell players and it would take silly money for him to leave this football club.'*

The manager is careful not to specify an exact hypothetical figure for this *silly money*, because to do so would constitute *slapping a price tag* on the player, hastening his departure considerably.

Unfortunately, the *'hands-off' warning* is inevitably subject to Isaac Newton's Third Law of Motion: for every action there is an equal – but opposite – reaction, which in this case can be found lurking in Stage 4.

Stage 4 – The loyalty pledge

Having obtained the manager's inadvertent assurance that the player will be leaving, the media then hunt down a statement from the player themselves. Influenced no doubt by their agent and, more heavily, by thousands of similar player statements in the past, the *in-demand ace* will, very probably, utter the following:

> *'I'm happy to stay at the club. I'm flattered by the interest, but it's all speculation. I'm a [Club X] player until told otherwise.'*

A sigh of relief for the fans then, but this statement still leaves open all possibilities. Again, any veteran of a *protracted transfer saga* should interpret this as a warning sign for the acceleration of the eventual deal – all pledges of loyalty are at risk of *dramatic U-turns*.

Stage 5 – The bid

Finally, contact is made and a bid lodged. At this stage, it is not uncommon for the bidding club to remain officially anonymous, but not essential. One near-guarantee is the reaction of the chairman of the player's club – the bid will almost always be dismissed as *derisory*. One of those words that you strongly sense those involved in football only know because of its use by those involved in football, *derisory* is the put-down of choice when it comes to opening bids. It also serves as a minor ego-boost for the smaller clubs, as a rare opportunity to look down their noses at the big boys.

Stage 6 – The 'come-and-get-me' plea

As outlined in Stage 3, the *'hands-off' warning* has an evil twin. It arrives in the form of the *'come-and-get-me' plea*. An even more awkwardly named cliché, the *'come-and-get-me' plea* is the clear declaration from the player that, despite the *derisory* opening bid, he now wants to leave the club, despite his earlier pledge of loyalty.

Perhaps rather a tabloid device, it's a common precursor for slapping in a written transfer request – verbal, emailed, texted, tweeted or carrier-pigeoned transfer requests are, regrettably, few and far between. While the bid rejection succeeds in at least stalling the inevitable, the club's reaction to their player's request to leave matters not a jot. For the record, though, the written transfer request is turned down.

In extreme cases, the selling club (for that is what they will surely be) banishes the player to train with the reserves or the

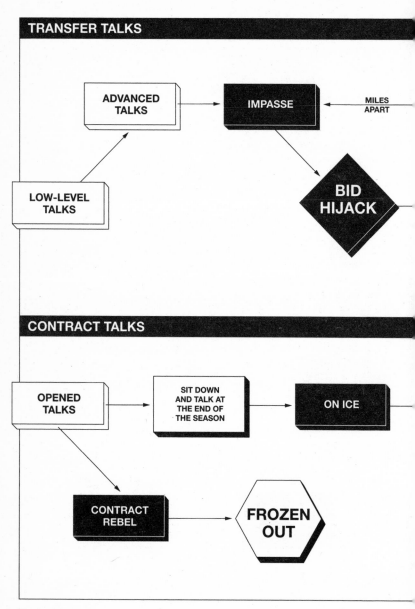

TRANSFER TALKS

ADVANCED TALKS → IMPASSE ← MILES APART

LOW-LEVEL TALKS → ADVANCED TALKS

IMPASSE → BID HIJACK

CONTRACT TALKS

OPENED TALKS → SIT DOWN AND TALK AT THE END OF THE SEASON → ON ICE

OPENED TALKS → CONTRACT REBEL → FROZEN OUT

The transfer saga

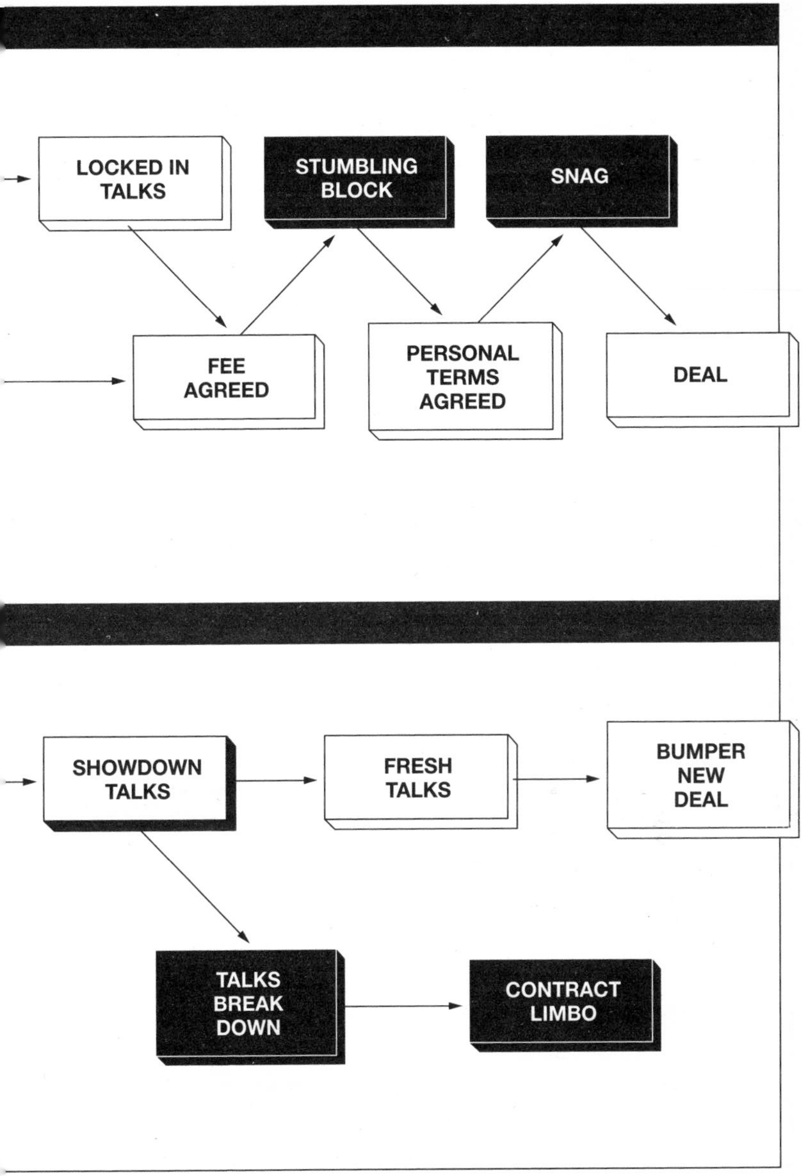

LOCKED IN TALKS

STUMBLING BLOCK

SNAG

FEE AGREED

PERSONAL TERMS AGREED

DEAL

SHOWDOWN TALKS

FRESH TALKS

BUMPER NEW DEAL

TALKS BREAK DOWN

CONTRACT LIMBO

youth team, a fate universally known as being *frozen out*. After this spectacular act of face-spite-induced nose removal, the club then prepares itself for the player's departure. Such a decision may indicate that the chairman/manager is a learned student of the *protracted transfer saga*, and recognises that resistance is futile.

As a side note, it must be added that this is a precarious, pivotal stage for the player. If they get injured and the deal collapses, the already *frozen-out* player will find themselves in the terrifying-sounding state of *transfer limbo*. The only viable way of escaping *transfer limbo* is to humbly withdraw the written transfer request and *knuckle down* once more.

Stage 7 – The negotiation

Now the two clubs are finally in dialogue over a possible deal, the *protracted transfer saga* would appear to be in full swing.

The two clubs must progress from *low-level talks* to *advanced talks*, at which point they become *locked in talks*.

It may then emerge that both parties are *miles apart* over the size of the fee, which constitutes a delay formally known as an *impasse*. As with any true saga, a potential twist is always on the horizon. It is at the *impasse* stage that the media begin to meddle. Reports of *bid hijacks* are rife, as other clubs are drawn into the melee. Usually perpetrated by a bigger club, and often conducted in the guise of a *swoop*, a perfectly executed *bid hijack* can leave rival fans fuming and your own supporters delighted in equal measure.

Stage 8 – Personal terms

With the fee agreed, the player is then liberated to discuss personal terms. Sky Sports News' persistence pays off, and a video of the player leaving the training ground in his car is looped endlessly. Despite this modern era of the greedy foot-baller, personal terms are still widely regarded as a *formality*, unless they prove to be a *stumbling block*.

The same also usually applies to the medical that the player must *undergo*. At this stage, the deal can be sealed – pending any unexpected, miscellaneous *snag*.

Stage 9 – The parade

At a press conference, the player is at last *paraded* and the new signing's ability to juggle a ball or hold up a replica shirt the right way round are given a severe test. This represents the first opportunity for the player to break his silence about the transfer, and the tried-and-tested statement is always worth the wait:

> *'I'm delighted to be here. As soon as I heard*
> *of [Club X's] interest, there was only one*
> *place I wanted to go. This is a massive club.'*

More brazen new signings go one step further and shamelessly try to profess boyhood support for their new club. Other variations include a player who has signed for a Championship club (particularly if he has left the top-flight to do so) describing his new employers as having *everything geared towards Premier League football*. This is a curious statement which seems to ignore the fact that the reason that the club looks like it is *geared towards Premier League football* is because it once was in the Premier League, but got relegated in pitiful fashion, crippled by debt and lumbered with a half-empty, albeit pristine, Lego stadium.

Stage 10 – The script

The *protracted transfer saga* reaches its conclusion (for strikers at least) with the player's return for a match against his previous club. Depending on how *acrimonious* his departure was, there will be much conjecture on the temperature of the reception he will face – he'll be hoping for a *warm reception*, but may find himself facing a *hot* one.

Anyway, egged on by *script*-wielding commentators, the player will inevitably get on the scoresheet on his return to his *old stomping ground*, a cue for the dreaded spectacle of the *muted celebration,* of course.

With the restrictions of UEFA's financial fair play rules finally taking effect, it's becoming less clear at which point a *transfer kitty* becomes a full-blown *transfer war chest*. The latter enables a club to embark on a wonderfully alliterative *summer spending spree*, during which they will face a multitude of *hands-off-warnings* and *come-and-get-me pleas*, while still claiming that they 'won't be *held to ransom* over [insert overpriced England international here]'.

Transfer budgets occupy a quaint corner of the football vernacular. Managers of lowly, unfashionable clubs must get by on the proverbial *shoestring* while billionaire owners are said to be funding lavish spending sprees by the rather old-fashioned method of *opening their chequebook*. Expensive strikers find themselves lumbered with a *hefty price tag* to go with the *monkey on their back*.

Amid all the chaos of the transfer window, just what do you get for your money these days?

£50k buys you a former shelf-stacker who's making quite a name for himself in the lower echelons of the *football pyramid*. He scored 48 goals last season for Hecklingborough Dynamo and you're confident that he can make the step up to the Football League.

For **£100k**, you're in the market for a *willing runner* from the League of Ireland with an eye for a goal. He'll be no respecter of reputations and, best of all, he'll fetch you a £5m profit when you sell him on to a mid-table Premier League side.

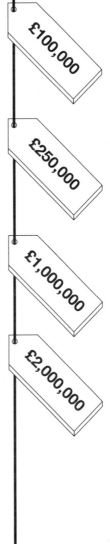

£250k is the pitiful amount due to clubs who nurture talent, only to see it *cherry-picked* by the *big boys*. If it's any comfort to the catchment-area gold-miners of League Two, even Barcelona have lost starlets elsewhere for a pittance.

£1m. A once-majestic figure that would be enough to capture the likes of Johan Cruyff or, erm, Trevor Francis. Now, you'll be lucky to snap up a promising League One defender.

Not so long ago, **£2m** would have been the going rate for a top-level performer. With football's superinflation, this is now a bargain-basement budget, but it's still a useful wad with which to delve under the radar for the Michu*s of this world*. In the cut-price Spaniard's case, his transfer fee has become the first ever algebraic football cliché, multiplied however many times to demonstrate the relative folly of, for example, signing a very old-fashioned English No. 9 for £35m (or seventeen-and-a-half Michu*s*).

£5m is now the RRP for a seasoned Championship goalscorer, who's good for twenty-five goals in the second tier but destined for a yo-yo existence after he misfires in the top flight. Students of the game know this as the Earnshaw Phenomenon, research on which many a parachute payment has been squandered.

For **£10m** you can secure the services of an all-purpose, *box-to-box midfielder* with international pedigree, but you'll have to sacrifice the optional extra of some goals.

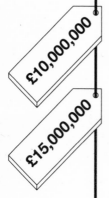

With **£15m** in his back pocket, though, a manager can indulge in a spot of impulse-buying at a major tournament, where a couple of eye-catching group-stage performances can earn a player a *money-spinning move* out of the *shop window* and into the Premier League.

The well-documented *English premium* is now set at **£20m**. As soon as a highly rated youngster makes his England debut in a meaningless June friendly, his club's ransom demand is permitted to reach these absurd levels. Inflated as it is, *the English premium* is only affordable for free-spending owners with more yachts than sense.

£30m is the minimum fee for an established, foreign-based superstar and the starting cost of making the mandatory *statement of intent* in the European transfer market ahead of the new season.

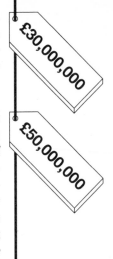

£50m represents the reserve price for an elite group of around half-a-dozen players in world football, who may only be *prised away* from their already illustrious employers by such *silly money*. The basis for transfer rumours involving these seemingly settled, successful players is the desperate need for something to write about in that May–August wasteland also known as *silly season*.

It's only a matter of time until a cheque for **£100m** is waved under the nose of Barcelona or Real Madrid. Until then, this figure exists purely as a deterrent buy-out clause. It's also, perhaps, a rather depressing number – what is left to capture the financial imagination after that? Some remember being glued to Ceefax in 1995 as Andy Cole's astronomical £7m fee for his move from Newcastle to Manchester United was emblazoned across the TV screen.

Nowadays, such a transfer bid would be downright *derisory*.

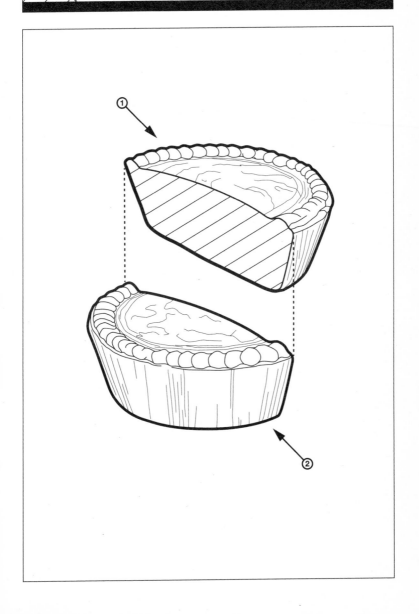

droves
/drəʊvz/

plural noun
1. herds or flocks of animals being driven in a body.

2. a sizeable group of football supporters leaving a match before it ends, having *seen enough*.

12. In Fine Voice:
Clichés of Football Fandom

To be a football supporter in 2014 is to be simultaneously caricatured by marketing minds, patronised by TV companies, pandered to by *beleaguered* managers and ripped off by pretty much everybody.

At the centre of all of that is the notion – perpetuated by all of the parties above, whatever their motivation – that football, without fans, would be nothing. Jonathan Wilson suggests this is misguided:

> *The idea that 'there'd be no game without the fans' is commonplace. There would; it's just it would be small-scale, played out on parks with nobody on the touchlines but the subs and a couple of bored players' girlfriends like most Sunday football. Sport doesn't need crowds to thrive; the likes of hockey, angling and rock-climbing get by perfectly well without thousands of people roaring encouragement or abuse at the participants.*[1]

Nevertheless, *giving the fans something to shout about* remains high on the list of priorities for down-on-their-luck sides and having them turn on you can prove as terminal for a struggling manager as *losing the dressing room*.

Inside a stadium, fans can gather in *pockets* and *smatterings* (often high up in the gods) or, if in greater numbers, can combine to form a *sea of blue/red/yellow, etc.* The length of the journey home for a travelling supporter is directly proportional to the number of goals their team concedes, further compounded by

1. From 'The Essential Backdrop' by Jonathan Wilson in *The Blizzard*, September 2012.

the unhelpful evening kick-off time and the British transport infrastructure. The various factors that combine to qualify a set of football fans as *hardy souls* can be expressed in the following formula:

$$\text{\textit{Hardiness of soul}}$$
$$=$$
$$\text{\textit{distance travelled}}$$
$$\div$$
$$\text{\textit{temperature}}$$
$$\times$$
$$\text{\textit{first-leg deficit (if applicable)}}$$
$$\div$$
$$\text{\textit{number of travelling support}}$$

Should a soul be hardened with sufficient frequency over time, the fan may then be described as *long-suffering*, exacerbating their need for that *something to shout about*. In lieu of shouting, they may still collaborate on a *chorus of boos* or the odd *howl of derision*, both of which a despairing manager will have no option but to sympathise with on the basis that *they pay their money and have every right* to make their feelings known. On better days, though, those fans may enjoy the dubious value for money of a piece of skill that was *worth the entrance fee alone*.

The traditional calendar of the football fan was, for decades, set in stone. The following exchange from the film adaptation of Nick Hornby's *Fever Pitch* summed it up perfectly:

> Sarah: 'So when does it all end?'
> Paul: 'May.'
> Sarah: 'And what happens then, in the summer?'
> Paul: 'Nothing. Boring. Just sit in the park and wait for the fixture list to come out.'

That may well have been the way of things in that scene's 1989 setting, but football has latterly managed to claim almost all of the previously barren summer wasteland. The publication of the fixture list, in isolation a mere administrative formality, has managed to retain its symbolism but the close season (for better or worse) is now a much more complex affair. In odd-numbered years, without the obvious appeal of a World Cup or European Championship, football can still occupy itself like never before.

The end-of-season review pieces are barely able to become fish-and-chip paper before the *transfer silly season* takes hold. Where transfer rumours could once only be gleaned from Teletext or (excruciatingly for holiday-goers) yesterday's newspaper, the last throes of May and the entirety of June are now the stage for minute-by-minute web coverage of *transfer sagas* and tense contract talks.

The release of the new season's fixtures must also compete with increasingly bombastic kit launches – each depicting various stern-looking squad members in incongruous settings (that is, anywhere but an actual football pitch), puffing out their sponsor-emblazoned chests. The new home kit is barely discernible from last season's. The away kit is promoted with some impenetrable marketing-department pseudoscience that claims that the space-age fabric lifts sweat from the body and filters it to produce drinking water. Finally, the deliberately lurid third kit is revealed (after having leaked via grainy warehouse photos on Twitter weeks before) for the purposes of horrifying purists everywhere.

There remains a window of a week or two where football fans must briefly rely on another sport for competitive stimulation – an Ashes series, a five-hour Wimbledon epic or, heaven forbid, some rugby – but football comes roaring back in mid-July in the form of a *money-spinning, lucrative Far East* market-exploiting, *gruelling* pre-season tour. And then, once the *traditional curtain-raiser* of the Community Shield is out of the way, we all have *something to shout about* once again.

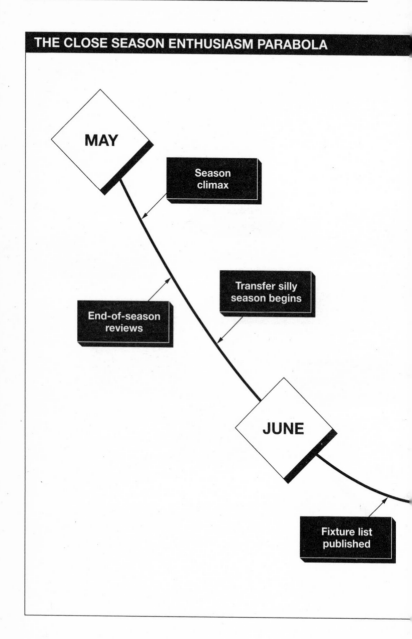

THE CLOSE SEASON ENTHUSIASM PARABOLA

MAY

Season climax

Transfer silly season begins

End-of-season reviews

JUNE

Fixture list published

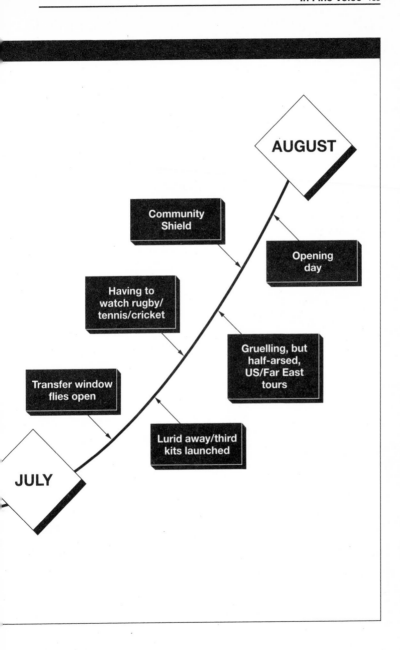

AUGUST

Community Shield

Opening day

Having to watch rugby/tennis/cricket

Gruelling, but half-arsed, US/Far East tours

Transfer window flies open

Lurid away/third kits launched

JULY

But what *do* we shout about? Amid the braying Schaden-freude inspired by the opposition's misfortunes, shoehorning various sentiments into the syllables of 'Sloop John B' by the Beach Boys and everything else under the umbrella of *terrace wit*, there remains a gem of spontaneity that unites all. This instinctive exclamation of glee, outside of the ultimate thrill of a goal, can only be transcribed as 'waaaaaaaaaaaaaaaaaeeeeeeeyyyyyyyyy!'

Usually a sign that the match is going your way (and, quite spectacularly, not the way of the opposing team and supporters), such an outburst is reserved for the more comical moments in the ninety minutes.

1. The referee falling over

A relatively rare example of when the whole stadium can justify joining in, the *Waaeey!* that ensues when the referee *goes to ground* is immediate and heartfelt. A truly classic *Waaeey!* and one that the official should accept in good humour.

2. An opposing player's pass goes astray

A fascinating example, as a misplaced pass goes into touch, and one which operates on a sliding scale:

Mild/relief
Relatively quick, sharp *Waaeey!* when a short pass eludes a full-back and exits the field of play.

Moderate/jovial
A long pass proves too high for a wide player and sails hopelessly over his head.

Strong/ridicule

A low pass slides away from the intended recipient and heads towards the touchline – but slowly enough to give hope of rescue. He chases the ball but narrowly fails to reach it and slides *unceremoniously* out of play, usually into advertising hoardings or, more excitingly, into the front row of opposing fans.

High/hysterics

The maximum attainable level on this scale since the backpass law was introduced. This occurs when a full-back's pass to a goalkeeper races towards the goal-line and out for a corner. The accumulative effect of flailing *custodian*, hands-on-head full-back, cheaply won corner, confrontation between said *custodian* and full-back and the resultant possibility of a scoring chance all mean that the maximum *Waaeey!* – in this context at least – is achieved.

The further up the scale, the more drawn out the *Waaeey!* becomes. A longer *Waaeey!* serves to highlight the increased calamity of the spectacle in question. Furthermore, the longer the *Waaeey!* the more pronounced the inflection at the end (*WaaaaaaaaaaaaaaeeeeeEEY!*), in a sort of final flourish of ridicule towards the target.

3. A second yellow card

While undoubtedly an expression of the pleasure at their team gaining a numerical advantage, the fans of the beneficiaries of the sending-off also wish to give the departing member of the opposition a fitting send-off. The referee assists here, acting as an unwitting conductor. The first yellow is shown, causing a ripple of recognition in the stands. Just as the crowd realise the implications, the red card is fished out of the pocket and they are given licence to *Waaeey!* as they wish. Spoilsport referees may opt to *brandish* the cards in quick succession. Although this succeeds in removing the rhythmic element of the *Waaeey!* it does little to stifle its fervour.

4. The ironic cheer

A unique example of a *Waaeey!*. This occurs when the referee is perceived to belatedly give the home side an overdue decision in their favour. Sarcasm is the highest form of terrace wit.

5. A shot that goes out for a throw-in

When a shot veers comfortably away from goal, there's a short but anxious wait to see which side of the corner flag it leaves play. Although not quite football's *ultimate indignity* – that remains the domain of the substituted substitute – but humiliating nonetheless.

6. Player hit in groin by football

An instantly identifiable event, notable for the player's crumpling to the ground in a manner that simply cannot be simulated, this is perhaps the cruellest of any *Waaeey!* Players getting struck in the *unmentionables* are a highlight for stadium and *armchair fans* alike, the latter even being treated to a slow-motion replay of the incident and some entry-level innuendo from the co-commentator.

7. An injury to a match official

Similar, of course, to a referee merely falling over, the *Waaeey!* here is accompanied by undoubtedly hilarious claims that he is in some way pretending to be injured (the 'irony' of which is too much for fans to resist).

8. A streaker

The invasion of a naked member of the public into proceedings, despite being one of those things that (arguably) *nobody wants to see*, is another prime candidate for a solid *Waaeey!* Indeed, depending on the success of the uninvited guest in evading the combined efforts of police and stewards, this incident can result in a multitude of *Waaeeys!* There's also around a 50 per cent chance that the co-commentator will observe how cold it is today, if you know what he means.

9. Manager controls the ball

Often the reserve of limelight-seekers such as Alan Pardew, this literal take on *kicking every ball* rarely fails to rouse the supporters into some semblance of a *Waaeey!*. Interestingly, both skilfully adept and comically bad attempts by suited and booted managers to retrieve the football in the technical area are greeted with the same approval from onlookers.

10. Assistant referee clattered by full-back

A linesman being inadvertently taken out by a full-back is a delightful sight. Unless a rare serious injury has been inflicted, the reaction of the assailant can range from sheepish schoolboy grin to all-out laughter shared with team-mates and opposition players alike.

One interesting conclusion can be drawn from incidents such as this. Despite spending ninety minutes berating the opposition, the opposition fans, useless members of their own team or the board, football supporters (if they are really honest) thoroughly enjoy sharing a light-hearted moment with everyone present. A moment that brings the whole ground together in spontaneous mirth should be applauded. The fact that sincere *hostilities are resumed* within seconds is even more brilliant.

Some mid-game sentiments cannot, however, be expressed purely by voice and require the support of quaint (but very, very earnest) A4-sized football banners (see page 190 for visual representation).

What first strikes you upon seeing these printed protests (usually against some perceived crimes against football administration) is the person holding it aloft. A middle-aged, stern-faced man. A middle-aged, stern-faced man who took the conscious decision before the game to conceive, type and print a message of protest on to a piece of A4 paper and take it with him to a football game, to hold it up for nobody in particular to read. Furthermore, the accessibility of A4-size paper notwithstanding, this man knew he'd need to get this banner on TV to have any chance of it being noticeable or legible to any more than half-a-dozen people. It is the minuscule size of these banners that set them apart from vandalised bedsheets in the cringeworthiness stakes.

Word processing advances have gradually phased out the hand-written A4 banner, which was often hampered by a misjudgment of the available space, leading to the last few letters having to be squeezed in by their (surely now crestfallen) amateur designer. A3-size paper is now increasingly common, saving those who really want to make their opinion heard the arduous task of printing two separate A4-size segments and taping them together, as if their dignity wasn't blown quite enough to smithereens.

We are yet to see the widespread use of iPad-based banners, which would offer the most fickle fans the real-time capability of targeting the overpaid underperformer of their choice, while the Etch-A-Sketch has survived over half a century without (to my knowledge) being used to declare someone a wanker at a Football League ground. But can these A4 banners do it on a *cold, wet Wednesday night in Stoke?*

Homemade, hand-held displays of allegiance do not necessarily have to be negative in their outlook. Tin-foil-and-cardboard FA Cups, which make up for their lack of bile in sheer preparation time, continue to be a vital component of *the magic of the FA Cup*. However, there has been a disappointing lack of progression to 3D forms, particularly given the malleability of the foil.

So, if you're sat at your computer on a Saturday morning, mulling over an A4-sized banner to take to your game that afternoon, give it some more thought. Really? Is it really worth it?

HOW TO MAKE AN ANGRY A4 BANNER

Newspaper cutting of intended target to avoid confusion

More than one colour suggests thoughtful preparation

Errant apostrophe

a4 BANNER'S OUT!!!

Multiple exclamation marks demonstrate passion

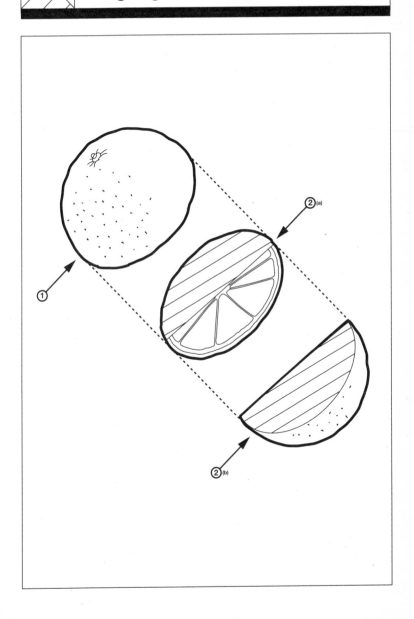

hoof
/huːf/

noun
1. the tip of a toe of an ungulate mammal, strengthened by a thick, keratin covering.

noun, verb *(informal)*
1. uncalculated, imprecise kick of a football in the general direction of the opposition goal and, more importantly, away from the kicker's own.

13. Where's the Talking?
The Language of Grassroots Football

Judging by countless television adverts, there is little in football that's more readily caricatured than Sunday league football. Pitiful playing surfaces, hangovers declared like trophies and polyester-testing physiques are only some of the overfamiliar tropes associated with the lowest rungs of the *football pyramid*.

While the facilities continue to dispirit many who turn out on a Sunday morning, the drip-down of mannerisms from the top flight, if not the funds, is in clear evidence. Skill levels are invariably at rock bottom, but this gap can be bridged to some extent by simply (and unconsciously) acting it out.

English football, from top to bottom, has always been characterised by its intangible, unquantifiable qualities of spirit, passion, the Siamese twins of *grit and determination* and, less notably, '*talking*'.

Talking is easy. Not talking enough is generally agreed in Sunday league to be highly counter-productive. Players are urged before kick-off for 'lots of *talking*', especially '*back there*'. Not talking is an accusation that can only be levelled at a whole team, rather than an individual (unless it is the captain, who must shout indiscriminately for ninety minutes, for that is his job.)

To avoid this indictment, a set of largely useless phrases has emerged, which can be called upon whenever necessary to punctuate a period of relative silence. Everyone knows them, everyone understands what they are vaguely supposed to mean, and almost nobody questions them.

Clichéd as they are, many strained bellows you hear on a football pitch – '*Man on!*', '*Out we go!*', etc. – are useful instructions. The following set of on-pitch *rallying cries*, however, deserve closer inspection:

1. 'We've gone quiet!'

Going quiet, as highlighted above, is the sign of a malfunctioning team. No one is talking, which means they all might as well go home. A period of notable quietness is ended only when the captain draws everyone's attention to it: '*Come on lads, we've gone quiet!*' It can, at the shouter's discretion, be bookended with '... haven't we?', to offer the illusion of a debate where one is really not available.

2. 'Straight in!'

A staple instruction that can be used only at a very specific moment – namely, the opponents kicking off the game. 'Run after the ball!', this phrase demands. 'Chase it when they kick it backwards!' Only the strikers need to do this, of course, and the moment quickly passes. Getting *straight in* is not a continuous requirement, but merely an opening gesture of intent, which is likely to be unfulfilled. It is instinctively accompanied by a mindless, yet somehow entirely appropriate-feeling, clap of the hands.

3. 'Two on the edge!'

When a corner is awarded, it is everyone's job to pick up their man. One eagle-eyed player has the extra task of spotting a discrepancy in this complex marking system, in that there are two unattended opponents lumbering into the penalty area.

In extreme circumstances, there may be *three on the edge* – an unthinkable catastrophe that is met with a suitably incredulous cry of '*I've got three here!*' The lack of concentration may be down to the defence's preoccupation with *the big man*, the lanky opposing centre-back/estate agent who has arrived with a look of great purpose from the back.

4. 'All day!'

An utterly irritating phrase (specifically designed to be so) used by smug opponents to declare your attacking efforts as weak and unlikely to succeed, even if repeated. Often said twice in quick succession – as a *speculative effort* flies into neighbouring allotments – to compound the humiliation.

5. 'It's still 0-0'

Football is an overwhelmingly childish pursuit. Much of football-supporting is based on Schadenfreude and suffering the taunts, in return, when your own team is humbled.

To combat this threat, some employ an overly defensive stance, hoping that an audible absence of pride will pre-empt any possible fall. And so, if the opposition races into an early lead, one stern-faced, armband-toting try-hard will attempt to construct a parallel universe in which the game is, in fact, goalless. '*The job is not done*,' he insists – a point he may return to when the final score is 7-4 or something similarly 1950s-era.

6. 'Box 'em in!'

A cult classic, perhaps, which satisfies two fundamental criteria: 1) a laughable attempt at tactical insight, and 2) exclaimed almost instinctively, every single time. The ball goes out for an opposition throw-in, deep in their final third, and it is universally accepted that they do not have the adequate technical skills (or simply the upper-body strength) to play/hurl their way to safety. This attritional passage of non-play frequently ends in a foul throw, which is generally regarded to be the most Sunday league thing imaginable.

7.'[Shirt colour] head on this!'

Possibly the most pointless one of all. For the uninitiated, this cryptic command is for your team-mates to meet an imminent opposition hoof with their head before the other lot can. No accuracy is necessary but congratulations are available for heading it really, really hard, straight back where it came from. '*WELL UP!*' you are told, with your name declared in full if the game is particularly tense. More forward-thinking pub-team players concern themselves with the second ball, which is often simply another header. Third balls remain an untapped, bewildering resource, possibly due to Chaos Theory.

8.'Away!'

Loosely translated as 'Now look here, team-mate, I neither want nor trust you to play your way out of trouble. Please dispose of the ball as quickly and as far away as possible.' Failure to do as directed leaves one open to castigation for '*fucking about with it there*', but this may be permitted if the player is in possession of a sufficient amount of...

9.'Time!'

The ball drops from the air and a player finds himself in acres of space. Pointing this out to him might seem a good idea. It'll calm him down, allow him to get his head up and play a pass, rather than treat the ball like an unpinned grenade.

However, when ten other players scream '*Time! Time!*' in unison, it tends to have quite the opposite effect. The futility of the situation is laid bare when, after giving away possession easily, the player is offered a final, withering, retrospective observation: '*You had time.*'

10. 'Anyone got any tape?'

The gold-dust of amateur football, despite being available in any hardware shop. As the sole provider of ankle-securing tape, once you declare and dispense it, you will never see it again. It also comes in handy for whichever team is on the wrong side of the most dreaded Sunday morning chore of all – putting the nets up.

11. 'Ref! Ref! How long?'

Usually asked by an overexcited player from the leading team, with surprising desperation. Whatever the answer, the player will always add about ten per cent on before relaying the revised figure to his team-mates.

12. 'Watch the short!'

It is considered a cardinal sin to let an opposing Sunday league team pass a goal-kick out to a full-back. Precisely what sort of blood-twisting tiki-taka an average pub team are expected to be capable of, deep in their own half, with the ball starting at the feet of the traditionally least capable player in their ranks, is anyone's guess.

Amateur-level goal-kicks, thumped aimlessly as far down the pitch as possible, aren't always a job for the goalkeeper. As the designated goal-kick taker for their sides, many amateur centre-halves can confirm that fetching a distant match ball in preparation for this moment is one of the more soul-destroying aspects of life at around 11am on every Sunday between September and May.

13. 'One of you!'

When a Sunday league midfield is instructed to '*get a [insert team's shirt colour] head on this*', you may then witness an unsightly clash of [insert team's shirt colour]-clad bodies as they simultaneously attempt to perform their primary duty. It is left to a team-mate to helpfully point out that only one of them was required on the scene.

14. 'Don't let it bounce!'

A rare example of a phenomenon that afflicts a Premier League side just as much as it does your grassroots rabble. Letting the ball bounce, especially *back there*, is traditionally asking for trouble.

15. 'Where was the shout?'

The ultimate act of Sunday league buck-passing. A player is *unceremoniously dispossessed* from behind, to *howls of derision* from his team-mates. Accompanied by a despairing flap of the arms, the player begs of his colleagues: '*Where was the shout?!*'

There wasn't one. Because they've *gone quiet*, haven't they?

The language of grassroots football

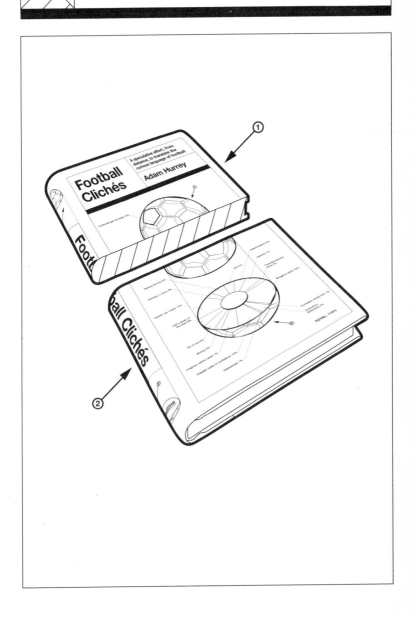

worldy
/wəːldli/

noun
1. short for world class. A goal, usually from long distance, of rare quality.

14. The Future of the Lexicon

What now for the football cliché?

If the game's increasing demand for high-quality coverage has led to its enhanced self-awareness, what chance is there for new words and phrases to mindlessly repeat their way into the football language? The sheer breadth of coverage – plus the actively encouraged contribution to it from fans – suggests a potential acceleration in the process by which a new entry can embed itself in the semi-conscious football dictionary. Up until 2004, buses existed in a football context almost exclusively for the purpose of being driven through the middle of disorganised, misshapen defences. Then, eight years after Arsène Wenger had introduced English football to futuristic things like pasta and not drinking alcohol, José Mourinho inspired the now-ubiquitous term of *parking the bus* to describe particularly unambitious, defensive performances. The successful (and relatively immediate) adoption of this phrase is partly explained by Mourinho's thrall, into which the press gladly fell on his arrival, but also simply because it did a concise job that no previously existing English football cliché could. That there might be football fans who are blissfully unaware of this particular decade-old phrase's origin serves to rubber-stamp its effortless encroachment into the lexicon. What this means for homegrown football clichés – 'tekkers' or 'worldy', to name but two – is unclear, but they still seem rather too raw to be considered a widespread automatic option.

After cold, wet Tuesday nights in Rochdale and *Wednesday nights in Stoke*, we are overdue a new English Capital of Footballing Culture. A wet Thursday night (on Channel 5, naturally) in Milton Keynes, perhaps?

As (I hope) this book has managed to convey, the football cliché is not limited to words on a page or from a broadcaster. Visual clichés – the *muted celebration* of Chapter 5, for example

– have blossomed at the same pace that 360-degree TV coverage has taken hold. At the most disposable end of their scale, some visual trends have a limited shelf-life: a celebrating John Terry has surely now been Photoshopped into every conceivable scenario and now social media must move on to its next natural resource. Twitter, in particular, is yet to establish itself as either a help or a hindrance to the future of the football cliché. On one hand, its currency of retweets seems a perfect environment for perpetuating accepted wisdom (*Arsenal trying to walk the ball in*, the uncorroborated concept of *international level*, the exaggerated significance of an *armband*). At the same time, though, football is now being satirised more than ever before and satire has no great patience for a cliché.

Whatever form they take, clichés remain a crucial part of football. *Football hipsters*, by their vague definition,[1] will never constitute the majority of fans, so everyone else still needs an accessible but stimulating way of consuming football coverage. The space-saving qualities of a perfectly poised football cliché remain important – we're post-Ceefax but still very much mid-Twitter – and there is little indication that footballers are more prepared to expand on the basic platitudes that have served their trade so uneventfully for decades. It's still *always nice to score*, but it's still *all about the three points*.

1. *The football hipster* is a slippery concept, but a predilection for progressive tactics, the Bundesliga and any historical national side who failed to win the World Cup are among its characteristics. And yet, once you've defined it, it must therefore become something else.

Acknowledgements

Thanks to my editor Richard Roper and everyone at Headline for their boundless enthusiasm, to Robert Hutton and David Hartrick for encouraging words and priceless feedback, to the designer James Edgar for bringing it all to life and to Paul Campbell at the *Guardian* and Thom Gibbs at the *Telegraph* for letting me write about football for money.